WHO — ME?
DO A PROGRAM?

Program Resources
For Congregational Events

CYNTHIA E. COWEN

CSS Publishing Company, Inc.
Lima, Ohio

WHO — ME? DO A PROGRAM?

Copyright © 1995 by
CSS Publishing Company, Inc.
Lima, Ohio

Library of Congress Cataloging-in-Publication Data

Cowen, Cynthia E., 1947-
  Who me do a program? / Cynthia E. Cowen
    p.   cm.
  ISBN (invalid) 0-7880-0590-1
  1. Activity programs in Christian education. 2. Worship programs. I. Title.
BV1536.C65 1995
259'.8—dc20   95-12243
                                             CIP

ISBN 0-7880-0590-1   PRINTED IN U.S.A.

To all those who cringe when they see me coming, I dedicate this resource. "Would you pray about being part of next month's meeting?" they hear me ask. "It's all written out — here's all you have to do." With less reluctance, they then take the program to look it over.

Who — Me? Do A Program? *is dedicated to all those who have presented these programs, but especially to the sisters in Christ at Christ the King Lutheran Church, Escanaba, Michigan, and Our Saviour's Lutheran Church, Iron Mountain, Michigan, who have brought life to each with their participation and giftedness.*

Table Of Contents

Introduction

It's newsletter time! Now, who's in charge of the next congregational program event? You are! Well, what are you planning on doing?

Who — Me? Do A Program? is a resource which will enable the person/group in charge to come up with meaningful program events for each month. Designed to be a 12-month resource, this program guide centers on such events as Valentine's Day, Saint Patrick's Day, Halloween, and other seasonal times. The programs are designed so that they may be used by women's organizations and youth groups, or as congregational fellowship and learning opportunities. They are arranged according to a yearly guide, but they may be used at any time where the program committee sees the need.

Leader's helps are included with each program resource.

Yearly Outline

January

1. God's Messengers Of Faith, Hope, And Love

Christmas is over, but God continues to bring us the message of salvation. This program uses three angelic messengers, Faith, Hope, and Love, to carry that message. The program may be done by a single individual who becomes each angel, or by a narrator and the three angelic messengers.

2. Blessed By God In Friendship

Friendships are gifts from God. This program explores the biblical friendships of Jonathan and David and Elijah and Elisha. It includes a narrator and six readers. A time of sharing special friendships is encouraged at the close of the program.

February

3. A Heart Filled With Love
February 14th is Valentine's Day. This program looks at the origins of this love-filled day. A narrator and four readers share a message from the heart filled with love. Three games are included for use before or after the program.

March

4. From Slavery To Sainthood!
Saint Patrick's Day is celebrated during this month, but who was this saint of old? This program traces Saint Patrick's journey from slavery to becoming the greatest missionary to Ireland. A leader and six readers make that journey real to the audience. Appropriate hymns and props are suggested.

April

5. Lenten Hopes
This program is subtitled "A Celebration of Lenten Disciplines." A reflector and seven readers examine various disciplines practiced during this church season. Topics covered are fasting, special commitments, alms-giving, study, prayer, and salvation. Lenten hymns are suggested.

May

6. Women Blessing Through Marriage
May is traditionally the time to recognize women in the church. This special program is designed to be used in connection with a bridal show. Participants are encouraged to write something special about their wedding day to be read while their dresses are modeled. Suggestions for the event are included to make it a festive occasion.

7. A Humorous Look At Some Hopeful Women

This program is another fun event for May or any other time of the year. It includes a narrator and six hopeful women: Eve, Mrs. Noah, Sarah, Paul's mother, Lydia, and Dorcas. Familiar songs have been adapted to be sung by the audience. Props and costuming are suggested. Humor is the mood of the program as the audience becomes more aware of these women who helped in God.

June

8. A Sundae Treat

It's getting warmer, and what more special way to encourage fellowship than to serve ice cream and the Word of God. "A Sundae Treat" is designed to be used as an afternoon event for youth or synod or as a program built around an ice cream social. Props are essential as the narrator builds a special banana split based on the Word. Illustrations for name tags and Bible study are included.

July

9. God's Picnic Basket

Congregations, youth or women like to picnic outdoors during the summer. This resource uses items you might take on a picnic. A leader and 13 readers share in building your own picnic event. Props and readings are listed.

August

10. The Armor Of God

School is just around the corner. The stores are loaded with the latest clothes styles which might not be around next year. "The Armor Of God" is that essential in the wardrobe of every Christian that never goes out of style. Done in the form of a fashion show, this program is based on Ephesians 6:10-17. A narrator introduces six models. A handout is provided and discussion on the skit encouraged.

September

11. Just Look At All Those Trees!

Fall colors are bursting forth as the trees begin to display God's beauty. This resource examines trees found in the Bible and what they represent. A narrator and six readers take the audience on a journey using visual props for emphasis. An excellent kick-off program for the start-up of any group.

October

12. In Pursuit Of The Right Spirit

Where did Halloween originate? Should Christians participate and encourage it? This program looks at the origins of this celebration and things associated with it like ghosts, hauntings, colors, fruit, and so forth. Sane Sara, the Saintly Saint, and Leapin' Lin, the Lover of Truth, use props and narration to guide the audience in their travels. Suggestions for decorations, fellowship, and games are included.

November

13. The Exodus Murmurers

November is pilgrim time. In ancient history, God has had his own pilgrims. This resource focuses on the exodus pilgrims and the murmuring they did. Participants include a leader, court reporter, and three Exodus Murmurers: Ms. Complaint, Ms. Grumble, and Ms. Murmur. Set in a court scene, a case is built against the three murmurers and a verdict solicited from the audience.

14. Where Do I Belong?

This resource is a means to share the purpose and mission of a group in your congregation. Wanda, the traveling "Women of the Church" reporter, visits a congregation and interviews an actress, a senior citizen, a bowler, and Connie Upreach, a congregational unit member. Good program for recruitment or educating others on one's organization. Props suggested.

December

15. Women Bearing Gifts

Set in the context of a worship service, this program looks at five women: Tamar, Rahab, Ruth, Bathsheba, and Mary, and the gifts they bring: The Gift of Righteousness, The Gift of Trust, The Gift of Unselfish Love, The Gift of Repentance, and The Gift of Obedience. Participants are encouraged at the close to offer their gifts to the Christ Child as an offering is taken.

1

God's Messengers Of Faith, Hope, And Love

Leader's Helps

This program is ideal for a January meeting of a women's group, youth event, or congregational fellowship night. It may also serve as an Advent or Christmas program since its three key characters are angels.

A leader introduces the program and each angel: the Angel of Faith, the Angel of Hope, and the Angel of Love. Each angel can dress with a different halo. Each wears a sign around her neck to tell which angel she is. If one person is doing the entire program, this switching of halos and signs enables that person to switch the characters.

Props

Angel of Faith: Halo, sign (Angel of Faith), and three signs which she puts up as she talks (1: Declare! Announce! Proclaim God's Promise, 2: To Rescue or Save God's Elect, and 3: To Bless).

Angel of Hope: Halo, sign (Angel of Hope), and three signs she puts up as she states those she visited (1: Gideon, 2: Manoah and Wife, and 3: Zechariah and Elizabeth).

Angel of Love: Halo, sign (Angel of Love), and three signs which wind up her talk (1: Let Faith Grow, 2: Receive God's Love — Jesus!, and 3: Hang Tight to Hope — Jesus!).

Additional

If time allows, the leader can bring forth three statues of angels representing Faith, Hope, and Love. She can invite participants to tell about people in their lives who have served as these angels, and how they brought them faith, gave them hope, and showed love.

Program

Leader: At Christmas time we sing carols such as "Hark! The herald **Angels** sing, glory to the new born king," or "**Angels** we have heard on high, sweetly singing o'er the plains." What about "It came upon the midnight clear, that glorious song of old, from **Angels** bending near the earth to touch their harps of gold"? And of course, "**Angels** from the realms of glory, wing your flight o'er all the earth. Once you sang creation's story, now proclaim Messiah's birth"? Christmas angels — spiritual beings; winged creatures singing God's praise; bringing tidings of peace and joy to all people. Medieval and Renaissance artists have pictured these beings as chubby cherubs with golden harps. But one must not be lulled into a limited vision of God's heavenly messengers and their mission. Most denominations recognize the ministry of angels among us as we celebrate Saint Michael and All Angels on September 29. The prayer for that day states that God has ordained and constituted the ministries of angels and mortals. This presentation will look at what that ministry might entail as we hear from three of God's heavenly messengers, Faith, Hope, and Love. Angel #1, would you introduce yourself and tell us a little bit about your ministry?

Angel of Faith: Hello. I am the Angel of Faith. Throughout history, God has been at work inspiring his people to have faith. He has sent angels as his messengers to speak in the authority of his name and to work wonders among his people. Now you may chuckle at the divine pictures of chunky cherubim in paintings or the graceful, female versions which adorn Christmas cards or tops of trees, but human beings do not really see us as we are. When we come to earth, we usually take on the form of a male human. No offense, girls, but

14

in all recorded instances of angels appearing to humankind, we have not taken the form of a woman yet. Today God is making an exception as I stand here before you to talk about my ministry of faith.

I was with two others as we came with a divine message in Genesis 18. Abraham was a great host, setting the example the writer of Hebrews reminds you to do as far as hospitality goes: "Do not forget to entertain strangers, for by so doing some people have entertained angels without knowing it" (Hebrews 13:2). We came to reveal the news that a son would be born to Abraham's wife, Sarah, within a year, and also to reveal that God's judgment was about to fall upon sinful Sodom and Gomorrah. That is the first part of my ministry — to declare, to announce, to proclaim God's promise (*sign*). A mixed blessing for those of faith. We like to hear good news even if it is far-fetched. Now Sarah looked at her body and her husband's and laughed at our announcement. They were too old. But remember, with God, all things are possible when combined with faith. Abraham looked at the twin cities of evil and grieved. Then he bargained with us to spare them if we could find ten righteous folk living there. What a limited view humans have of God's grace. God knows the heart. He knew that when two of us entered the city, evil men would even seek to sexually assault us. There actually was only one good person in that city, Lot, Abraham's nephew, and we did rescue him.

The second part of my ministry is to rescue or to save God's elect (*sign*). We reached out our hands and pulled Lot in from those who sought to harm him and us. Then we led him, his wife, and two daughters out before destroying the town. We told them not to look back, but sometimes humans do not listen to us. Lot's wife didn't. Her curiosity got the most of her, and she turned to look. At once she became a pillar of salt. There are dire consequences when you choose to disobey God's voice. What God promises to do, he will do, yet he will have mercy on those who are in right relationship with him.

15

Faith is a key part in the story of Abraham and Sarah. Sarah tried to secure that son for herself by giving her Egyptian maid, Hagar, to her husband. Remember that Old Testament story? That affair only caused trouble as Sarah took matters into her own hands. I was sent twice to Hagar. The first time with an announcement that her child would become a mighty nation, and she was to call him Ishmael. Of course, since this child was not the child of Promise, he would be at odds throughout the centuries with the true heir of Abraham, Isaac. Today you see this with the factions of Muslims (the sons of Ishmael) warring against Jews and Christians (the sons of Isaac). When the promise of a son was realized, and Isaac was born, Sarah had Abraham expel the slave girl and her son from their midst, but God sent me to rescue them in chapter 22. Abandoned in the desert, Hagar set the boy aside so she would not see him die. She cried out, and God sent me once again to instill faith into her grieving spirit. I opened her eyes to her surroundings, and she saw water. It had always been there, but in her grief and pity, she did not see it. How true this is of most people. They become blinded by circumstances and do not see God's presence in the midst of difficulty. Yet God is faithful and will rescue those who cry out to him.

But God was not finished with my ministry of instilling faith in Abraham's life. For when God asked Abraham to sacrifice his son, Isaac, I was present. By faith Abraham had believed he would have a son. By faith he believed that God would even raise this son from the dead if need be to fulfill the promise God had made with him of making him a great nation. I called out to Abraham on that mountain and stopped him from killing Isaac. That is when I performed my third part of ministry — to bless (*sign*). Since Abraham had demonstrated great faith in not withholding his son, I was given the authority from God to bless him and to make his descendants as numerous as the stars of heaven and as the sand on the seashore. You are the heirs to that blessing. God has planted faith in your hearts. He has given you a promise in baptism — to become his child. He has rescued you from the power of sin and death. All who turn to his Son, Jesus, who was our ultimate sacrifice, and believe in him as Lord and Savior, God blesses with eternal life. Receive my ministry among you today. Hear by faith the promise, allow God to rescue you from sin and whatever difficult situation you may be in, and be blessed with his presence. Stretch your faith today and see God perform miracles in our midst. Shalom.

Leader: Let us now hear from our second messenger from God, the Angel of Hope.

Angel of Hope: It is very exciting to be with you today. I am the Angel of Hope. What a privilege it has been to be sent forth from God to inspire and instill hope in his people. I especially like to come to people who see no way out of their dilemmas.

One of those I visited was Gideon (*sign*). It was fun to sit under that oak tree at Ophrah and watch the young Hebrew beating out wheat and then hiding it from his enemies, the Midianites. When I brought him greetings from the Lord, he was perplexed and asked, ''If the Lord is with us, why then has all this happened to us?'' God had promised to be with Israel, but the nation had sinned. They needed a deliverer. I was there 1 — to instill once more God's promise of hope; and 2 — to rescue and deliver Israel from the hands of their enemies. Humans often lose sight of God's promise in the midst of dire straits. Gideon and his people had. But God sent me to commission this young warrior. His response was normal, ''How can I deliver Israel? My clan is the weakest in Manasseh, and I am the least in my family.''

But remember, with God all things are possible. Maybe you've cried out like Gideon for help. Then when God says, ''It's time to stop praying and to start acting,'' your response is, ''Who? Me, Lord? You can't mean I'm to do it? I'm not able.'' That's when I come to give you hope for it's not by your own power but the power of Christ in you that you can accomplish what God has called you to do.

17

Of course, Gideon needed his faith bolstered so he asked for a sign that God's favor was with him. So I provided it. I touched his offering with my staff and fire leapt out to consume it. He was impressed, to say nothing of his fear of having seen an angel face to face. Those face-to-face encounters do startle mortals.

I remember the time God sent me on another assignment: to bring hope to Manoah and his wife (*sign*). They were childless, and God sent me to bring the good news that they would have a son, Samson, who would be powerful like Gideon and rescue his people from their enemies. I planted hope in their hearts, and they were good parents.

Their son, Samson, however, was a different case. If God simply relied on loyal angels, how smoothly things would run. But God chooses mortals through whom to work, and sometimes they do stray from his paths. However, even after Samson had been seduced and betrayed by Delilah, and captured and blinded by the Philistines, God did not abandon him. God's promise to be with us to the end is something we can trust in. He had rescued the couple from their childless state and blessed them with a mighty son and judge over Israel. What a sign to heathen nations as the chained and blind Samson once again demonstrated God's power as God restored his strength! The Philistines were crushed as he toppled the pillars of their temple.

That reminds me of another childless couple I was sent to give hope to and confirmed it with a sign. Zechariah and Elizabeth (*sign*), an old couple like Abraham and Sarah, and Manoah and his wife, were childless. God sent me to Zechariah to bring hope. I made him a promise that his wife would bear a son. Of course, he didn't believe so I gave him a sign. He would remain mute until the day God's promise was fulfilled. John the Baptist, their son, was a blessing to an entire generation as he prepared the way for Jesus' ministry.

It is exciting to see how hope springs up within God's people to believe in his promises, to respond to his love and to be rescued from enemies or situations like childlessness, economic difficulties, and so forth. God knows your deepest need and is waiting for you to call out to him. What blessings occur when you open yourself up to my ministry among you of bringing hope! May the hope planted in your hearts today carry you through times of difficulty as well as times of joy as you trust in God and Christ Jesus, his Son. Shalom.

Leader: The Angel of Faith and the Angel of Hope have both told us of the three-fold ministry they have of declaring God's promise to us, of rescuing us, and of blessing us. Let us hear what the Angel of Love has to say.

Angel of Love: 1 Corinthians 13:13 states that "faith, hope and love abide, but the greatest of these is love." Now I don't negate the ministry of my two friends, Faith and Hope, but I do know that we all work together to bring God's message of love to the world. God has been with his people since the beginning of time when he chose them to be his people. He sent me to Moses and look what happened. All those wonders astounded the Egyptians. I declared God's message of love and promised to be with them, to deliver them, to rescue them out of their bondage. God did it.

Then the Lord blessed them by sending me before them in a cloud by day and a pillar of fire by night. In Exodus 23 God told Moses specifically that he would send an angel to guard them on their way to the Promised Land because he loved them. They were to be attentive to me and listen to my voice. Their enemies would be defeated if they obeyed me. They would be blessed for their faith and hope as they trusted in God's promise to be with them. Of course, we all know they never received their full inheritance because of sin and unbelief. I did my best at ministering to them. Battles were fought, and the heavenly hosts of heaven did supernatural things. Satan had a field day at times, but with God in control, the victory is sure.

God sent me to minister love to his own Son. After all those temptations, Jesus had the victory but was exhausted in the wilderness. The Lord quickly dispatched me to minister love.

No one likes wilderness experiences. The Israelites didn't, Jesus didn't, and I'm sure you don't. But they are faith-building times, and there is hope in them, for God is there in the wilderness with us.

And the good news is that his love does not stop — even if ours does. Look at the Garden of Gethsemane. Jesus cried out to God to take the cup of suffering away, but asked that not his will but God's be done. God sent me to be with Jesus to minister the Father's love and to bring him strength for what was ahead. Even on the Cross, Satan cried out to Christ, "He rescued others, but he can't save himself." The host of angels stood ready to wipe the mockers out, but God loved the world so much that he allowed Christ to suffer and die that all who believe in him might have eternal life. That is your promise. That is your rescue from the power of sin. That is your blessing.

What a joy it was to greet Mary Magdalene in the garden that Easter morning. She had never seen an angel, but I appeared to her to recall God's promises that he would rise and bless others with the Good News of salvation. All because God loved him. Jesus loved Mary and chose to reveal himself to her.

Jesus loves you and has chosen to reveal himself to each of you through the power of his Spirit. He has made you a promise — that when you turn from your sin and receive him as Lord, he will rescue you and forgive your sins. Jesus will bless you with new life as you surrender yourself unto him.

Let the three of us minister God's gifts of faith, hope, and love in your lives today. Let **Faith** grow (*sign*), hang tight to the **Hope** you have in Jesus (*sign*), and receive God's **Love** poured out in Jesus' death and resurrection (*sign*). Call upon Jesus to be with you daily and for us to be there also, for God sends his angels to minister to those he loves. May the joy of God be with each of you today and forevermore. Go in the peace of the Lord and under the protection and ministry of his angels. Amen.

2

Blessed By God In Friendship

Leader's Helps

All of us desire to have and to be good friends. True friendships are to be valued as gifts from God. "Blessed By God In Friendship" is a program which explores two biblical friendships: Jonathan and David; Elijah and Elisha.

This program can be used by different groups in the church to help the participants become aware of what true friendship can be.

Those involved in this program are one leader and six readers. The readings for the readers are listed below.

Reader 1: 1 Samuel 14:6-7

Reader 2: 1 Samuel 17:45-47

Reader 3: 1 Samuel 18:1-4

Reader 4: 2 Samuel 1:23-26

Reader 5: 1 Kings 19:19-21

Reader 6: 2 Kings 2:1-12

The program closes with the hymn, "What A Friend We Have In Jesus."

Program

Leader: What a treasure is found in one who has a Christian friend! Truly there is no greater blessing that can be given to one than a friend who remembers us in daily thoughts and prayers, who shares our happy and sad times, who knows the best and worst of us, and who loves us in spite of our faults. A true friend is a gift from God. It is as if God's finger reaches out and touches our lives in a special way when we make a friend in Christ. Emerson said that friendship was like immortality — too good to be believed. The writer of Ecclesiasticus tells us that "a faithful friend is a strong defense, and one that has found that friend has found a treasure" (Ecclesiasticus 6:14).

Too often in life, we go about our business living not in "true friendship" with others but merely in surface relationships. However, friendships are not just something we take out when we need them. They need to be cultivated and nurtured in love. It takes time and commitment to be a true friend, but as we invest in other people, we are blessed in so many ways. As we share with another person and love him or her as a friend, we also feel and experience God's love. This program will explore the blessing of experiencing God through friendship by looking at the relationship of two special friendships found in God's Word. The first is David and Jonathan, the soldier and the prince. The second is Elijah and Elisha, the prophet and the apprentice.

Now Jonathan was the son of Saul, who had been anointed by the prophet Samuel in God's name to be king over Israel. During his father's rule, Jonathan won a reputation for himself as a mighty warrior. He was not a pompous prince who stayed at home, but one who accompanied his father into battle as a leader. At times the impetuous youth took many chances that made his father and elders cringe. In 1 Samuel

13 and 14 we see recorded a battle where only Saul and Jonathan had spear and sword. The 600 Israelites who accompanied them had only their fists and shepherd staffs with which to fight the Philistines. Yet in spite of the odds and helplessness of the situation, Jonathan set out to spy on the enemy with only his armor-bearer. The wisdom of his decision probably would have been questioned, so he did not inform his father about what he planned to do.

We read in 1 Samuel 14:6-7 of some of the qualities of friendship this young man embodied which we might want to cultivate in our own lives.

Reader 1: "Jonathan said to the young man who carried his armor, 'Come, let us go over to the garrison of these uncircumcised; it may be that the Lord will act for us; for nothing can hinder the Lord from saving by many or by few.'

"His armor-bearer said to him, 'Do all that your mind inclines to. I am with you; as your mind is, so is mine' " (1 Samuel 14:6-7).

Leader: Now Jonathan was one of those people who inspire loyalty among their comrades. In war they are called "foxhole buddies." When we are in personal jeopardy, we tend to develop close relationships with those around us who challenge us to have faith and trust. Jonathan was one such as this. His armor-bearer was with him heart and soul, a bonding that said, "I'll follow where you lead because I trust in your leadership."

Yet Jonathan had a higher trust. He was not looking at his own abilities to save the day but to God who would act on his behalf. The free-for-all that took place found the two Israelites killing some 20 men. The panic, which then ensued in the camp of the Philistines, sent the enemy fleeing. It was a panic sent by God. The Lord rescued Israel that day not because they were in a sad state, but because of Jonathan's boldness to trust that God would deliver. Jonathan surveyed the situation, planned accordingly, placed his hope and trust

23

in God, and set out guided by the Spirit. Following this example we, too, will experience God's victory in our lives.

Another who had this fearless trust in God was David. David, a shepherd boy whom God anointed king because of Saul's disobedience, displayed similar characteristics to Prince Jonathan. He was young like the king's son. He was impetuous and didn't count the odds against him. He was courageous as he looked at the giant, Goliath, and decided that the man had to be taken on. Taking only his sling and five small pebbles, David approached the Philistine with boldness and trust in God. In 1 Samuel 17:45-47 we read of his challenge.

Reader 2: "But David said to the Philistine, 'You come against me with sword and spear and javelin, but I come to you in the name of the Lord of hosts, the God of the armies of Israel, whom you have defied. This very day the Lord will deliver you into my hand, and I will strike you down and cut off your head; and I will give the dead bodies of the Philistine army to the birds of the air and the wild animals of the earth, so that all the earth may know that there is a God in Israel, and that all this assembly will know that the Lord does not save by sword or spear; for the battle is the Lord's and he will give all of you into our hand' " (1 Samuel 17:45-47).

Leader: We all know the outcome. David took aim and killed the giant. Victory came from God in whom David had put his hope and trust.

Jonathan and David had many things in common which would form a foundation for their friendship. They were both warriors, courageous in battle, young, adventuresome, leaders, not afraid of the odds against them, and wise in their dealings with those around them, especially their immediate families. But the one thing that bound them even tighter in friendship to each other was their trust and faith in God. God's Spirit was with them both, empowering them to do his will and creating a bond of friendship that was eternal. Hear what happened after David had killed Goliath.

Reader 3: "When David had finished speaking to Saul, the soul of Jonathan was bound to the soul of David, and Jonathan loved him as his own soul. Saul took him that day and would not let him return to his father's house. Then Jonathan made a covenant with David because he loved him as his own soul. Jonathan stripped himself of the robe he was wearing, and gave it to David, and his armor, and even his sword and his bow and his belt" (1 Samuel 18:1-4).

Leader: We have recorded in these verses a "classic" friendship. Exchanging one's armor or clothing was a common way of sealing a friendship. Jonathan saw in David a person like himself. God's Spirit quickened his heart, and he responded. Not waiting for an overture on David's part, Jonathan reached out to his new friend and was blessed. Later David became not only a resident in Jonathan's father's home but actually married into the family when Saul gave his daughter, Michal, to David in marriage. Sharing blood family relationships enhanced their friendship bond, but it was even stronger than blood for it caused Jonathan to take sides with David against his own father.

Saul, who had become very jealous of David's influence with the people and his victories in battle, tried many times to kill his son's friend. David fled the court and hid from Saul. Jonathan went as an encourager to show his friend that he was on his side. This was a sign of a deep and committed friendship.

There may be times when we are called to stand with a friend against a blood family member's error in judgment or an envious spirit. This may be difficult for many of us, and so we need to recall that Jonathan loved his friend with a love that crossed family lines and went beyond his own desires. David would be the next king of Israel, not Jonathan to whom succession to the throne would have passed. Jonathan would have given up the throne for the friendship he experienced with David. He knew that David had been ordained by God to guide the nation he might have ruled.

25

Jonathan and David admired each other. They trusted each other with their lives. But the foundation of their trust and love was not in the surface relationship of friendship but based on their trust and love of God who had brought them together. This is seen as David grieves the death of his friend Jonathan and his king Saul as seen in 2 Samuel 1:23-26.

Reader 4: "Saul and Jonathan, beloved and lovely! In life and in death they were not divided; they were swifter than eagles, they were stronger than lions. O daughters of Israel, weep over Saul, who clothed you with crimson, in luxury, who put ornaments of gold on your apparel. How the mighty have fallen in battle! Jonathan lies slain on your high places. I am distressed for you, my brother Jonathan; greatly beloved were you to me; your love to me was wonderful, passing the love of women" (2 Samuel 1:23-26).

Leader: In this passage we hear a cry of one who loved with a deep love as a result of experiencing God's love in friendship. The gift God had given him of a brother in faith was one which had to be mourned. And we, too, will mourn those we have loved knowing that one day we will be reunited in Christ.

The example of friendship we first looked at showed how easy it was for two people to form a relationship based on similar age and family relationships, similar occupations, similar personalities, and similar environments. But what about those situations where God calls us to form friendships with persons not like us in any way? Let's look at an example from 1 Kings 19:19-21.

Reader 5: "So he set out from there, and found Elisha, son of Shaphat, who was plowing. There were twelve yoke of oxen ahead of him, and he was with the twelfth. Elijah passed by him and threw his mantle over him. He left his oxen, ran after Elijah, and said, 'Let me kiss my father and mother, and then I will follow you.' Then Elijah said to him, 'Go back again; for what have I done to you?' He returned from following him, took the yoke of oxen, and slaughtered them; using the equipment from the oxen, he boiled their flesh, and gave it to the people, and they ate. Then he set out and followed Elijah, and became his servant" (1 Kings 19:19-21).

Leader: Here we see God's call to two unique and different individuals to form a friendship relationship based entirely on God's decision. Elijah had been a prophet, or spokesperson for God, for some time now. His ministry has had an Alice-in-Wonderland style. Calling down a three-year drought and bringing rain once more, raising the dead son of a widow, challenging the prophets of Baal and calling down fire from heaven to consume a drenched offering, traveling alone, speaking out against the king and his wicked queen, fleeing for his life, being fed by ravens and hearing God's voice in a cave — all these incidents tend to conjure up for us an image of a very strange man doing his thing alone yet under the mysterious moving of the Almighty.

One of the key characteristics of this man of God was his obedience. So, when God told him to go and find this young Elisha, he went. The placing of the mantle upon the young farmer's shoulders signified the call of God and the transfer of power. With no further explanation or ado, Elijah turned to leave. The young boy, desiring closure to his former life, asked permission to say farewell to his family. Matter of factly, the prophet told him that he knew he had been called and to do what he felt he had to do. In other words, "You know, Elisha, that I, the prophet of the Most High God, have just anointed you in his name and transferred the mantle of power onto your shoulders. You have been called into his service. Now the ball is in your corner. Goodbye!"

This is truly a strange way to begin a friendship. No love of brother is expressed like that of Jonathan for his new friend David who had just killed Goliath. No admiration. No thrill of victory. Elisha was busy with everyday life when God called. The man of God appeared, did his thing, and turned to go his way. Emotion welled up for those the young man would leave so he entreated the prophet to allow him some time to make the parting easier. But the elder seemed to be less than understanding as he stated the plain facts: "Listen, lad. God told me to anoint you. If you want to follow, get yourself set and come." The boy must have wondered if the old man had any family ties. To whom did he say goodbye, or did he?

Unlike the disciples who left their nets immediately when Jesus called, Elisha took time to say goodbye to family and friends. They were important to him. Before he could begin to walk with God and this new "friend," he wanted to say farewell. He prepared himself emotionally to enter into a new relationship. He prepared himself spiritually as well, offering up sacrifice to God. This could be an important step for each of us to consider when looking at entering new realms of call.

After Elisha had completed his task and said goodbye, he walked with Elijah, learning from him and taking care of the man's needs. Now we might ask ourselves what type of friendship could develop between these two dissimilar people? The answer is a friendship based on God's calling to serve one another. The older, wiser prophet was to teach and instruct the younger novice in the ways of the Lord. The younger was to be a companion and student of the other. As they walked the dusty roads and shared their meals, as they prayed and read the scriptures, as they lived in continued obedience to the call of God, their friendship grew.

In Bethel there were many others seeking the Lord also. They supported and encouraged one another in community. Elijah, the senior prophet at the time, knew his time had come. God was about to take him away, and the prophet made this very plain to his apprentice and friend. We hear this story in 2 Kings 2:1-12.

Reader 6: "Now when the Lord was about to take Elijah up to heaven by a whirlwind, Elijah and Elisha were on their way from Gilgal. Elijah said to Elisha, 'Stay here; for the Lord has sent me as far as Bethel.' But Elisha said, 'As the Lord lives, and as you yourself live, I will not leave you.' So they went down to Bethel. The company of prophets who were in Bethel came out to Elisha, and said to him, 'Do you know that today the Lord will take your master away from you?' And he said, 'Yes, I know; keep silent.' Elijah said to him, 'Elisha, stay here; for the Lord has sent me to Jericho.' But he said, 'As the Lord lives, and as you yourself live, I will not leave you.' So they came to Jericho. The company of prophets who were at Jericho drew near to Elisha, and said to him, 'Do you know that today the Lord will take your master way from you?' And he answered, 'Yes, I know; be silent.' Then Elijah said to him, 'Stay here; for the Lord has sent me to the Jordan.' But he said, 'As the Lord lives, and as you yourself live, I will not leave you.' So the two of them went on. Fifty men of the company of prophets also went, and stood at some distance from them, as they both were standing by the Jordan. Then Elijah took his mantle and rolled it up, and struck the water; the water parted to the one side and to the other, until the two of them crossed on dry ground. When they had crossed, Elijah said to Elisha, 'Tell me what I may do for you, before I am taken from you.' Elisha said, 'Please let me inherit a double share of your spirit.' He responded, 'You have asked a hard thing; yet, if you see me as I am being taken from you, it will be granted you; if not, it will not.' As they continued walking and talking, a chariot of fire and horses of fire separated the two of them, and Elijah ascended in a whirlwind into heaven. Elisha kept watching, and crying out, 'Father, father! The chariots of Israel and its horsemen!' But when he could no longer see them, he grasped his own clothing and tore them in two pieces'' (2 Kings 2:1-12).

Leader: The time had come for Elijah to cease his labor for the Lord. His ministry on earth had been powerful. His guidance to younger prophets had left its mark — especially on Elisha. The younger would not leave the older. This is a wonderful illustration of ''devoted'' friendship which we see in the biblical friendship stories of Joshua and Moses, Jonathan and David, and Ruth and Naomi. This devotion is born of God and embedded in the human character rising to shine in some outstanding friendship bonds. It crosses conditions and race. It crosses age and desires.

When the older prophet first met the younger, Elijah knew that the other would go on under God's anointing to also do ministry. Elijah was not bitter that God would end his ministry and raise Elisha's. He was not jealous of the youth's potential and life ahead. His friendship for the other honored God's call and will. John the Baptist recognized this also when he realized that his ministry was about to come to an end with the advent of Jesus on the scene. He had prepared the people for this very thing, and he stepped aside so Christ would have prominence.

Often friendships are too easily broken. Loyalties, when tested, break down. Self-interest takes the place of selfless devotion. Feelings are wounded. We see a good example of this in Saint Paul when Barnabas insisted that Mark accompany Paul and Barnabas on their second missionary journey. Paul, having been abandoned by Mark once before, was not about to take the chance again. Angry words were exchanged, and Barnabas left with Mark for Cyprus while Silas accompanied Paul. In time, the hurt was healed by the one who bound these friends together — God — but at the time the separation of friends was painful. Mark went on to write the Gospel of Mark on that island, and years later was reconciled to Paul and was with him as a brother in the Lord's service.

The love and devotion that Elisha had for his master is seen as he calls out, "My father! My father!" as Elijah is swept up in a chariot of fire. He rends his garments as a sign of his grief, but then picks up the mantle and carries out the role now assigned to him. Elisha would never measure up to the greatness of his master, but his prophetic career reminds us that without great capacities, without being a hero, one can still do much good in the world. Elisha served God in daily life but remembered the greatness of his old friend. He did not become down and dumpy because he couldn't have a "fire and water" ministry like Elijah's. God had called him to service in a different way, and as long as God was present, he would rejoice in that call, drawing from memory the times of friendship with one greater than he.

Have you raised anyone from the dead? Have you parted any waters lately? Have you heard God speak in the stillness of the night? Have you heard a distinct call to service from God? Do you have a friend in Jesus? Do you have the Spirit's anointing and power? Have you experienced the love of God shown for us this day?

As we open ourselves up to experiencing all God desires for us as his children, we will receive blessings as we allow God to form our friendships and develop them in Christ. Friendship based on God's call and open to his refining is a valuable treasure.

Yet there is another friend whom God will bless us with if we but seek his love. An old hymn, "What A Friend We Have in Jesus," states it well.

As we close this time together by singing this song, let us remember that friendships based on the things of this world are good for a time, but when the experience is over, the friendship doesn't have the same depth of commitment. Friendships called by God and blessed by his love and presence will continue, for it is the Christ we see in the other that keeps that friendship alive.

Let us conclude our program by asking God to bless us with his presence in all our friendships, and by asking that we would be open to his call when he issues it to be a friend to another — for we never know the surprise in store for us as we say, "Lord, I'll reach out in your love. Help me to be the friend you desire to this person."

May we be blessed with friendship's blessings and enjoy the warmth of understanding, the comfort of companionship, and the joy of appreciation.

Sing "What A Friend We Have In Jesus."

(If time allows, have participants share their feelings concerning the blessings of friendship based in Christ and a friend in whom they have seen Christ.)

3

A Heart Filled With Love

Leader's Helps

This February Valentine program is designed for use in the congregation by a youth, women's or intergenerational group or by a couple's club. Based on the theme of love, "A Heart Filled With Love" uses four readers and four verses of the hymn, "Love Divine, All Loves Excelling," to share the history of Saint Valentine and the evolution of Valentine's Day. Each reader wears a heart with the corresponding letters **L-O-V-E** printed on it. At the conclusion of the program, the four readers stand together spelling out the word, LOVE. Three games are included which may be used before or after the program. A paraphrase version of 1 Corinthians 13 is suggested for a devotional reading. Decorations may follow the valentine theme.

Program

A Program For Valentine's Day

Verse 1 of "Love Divine, All Loves Excelling"

Reader 1 (*Wears a valentine with letter L on it*): February 14 is the day on which we celebrate one of our oldest holiday traditions here in America: Saint Valentine's Day. Historians are not sure who Saint Valentine actually was. Legend has it that he was a Roman citizen of the third century who had found faith in the one true God. When Christianity began to spread throughout the Roman Empire, becoming an irritant to those in power, it became convenient for the Emperor to blame Christians for Rome's troubles. A decree was issued by Emperor Claudius against those practicing this "new" religion. Many were arrested for their conversion to faith to this new god called Jesus. The cost for many was high as the prisons became filled with Christians, and the arenas became death pits for believers as gladiators and wild beasts put an end to their earthly lives. This new way of loving one God and your neighbor was strange, threatening, and unsettling to the hearts of many Romans.

However, Valentine was one Roman who had a heart filled with love and a hope in Christ. Having embraced the Good News of salvation, it is said that he reached out in love to those around him. His new faith touched many and brought them hope of a life hereafter. Children became the special object of that love just as they were to his Lord and Savior. Even during his imprisonment, his heart reached out to his captors. The prison keeper's daughter was said to have been healed of blindness by Valentine. The Spirit of Christ's love could not be restrained even behind bars as many were touched by this miracle. But Valentine was killed for his faith by decree of the Emperor, and Saint Valentine emerged as a Christian martyr. But what is the connection to Saint Valentine and the day which has evolved as we know it?

Reader 2 (*Wears a valentine with the letter* O *on it*): Thousands of years ago the Romans celebrated a holiday known as Lupercalia, the "feasts of Lupercus." Lupercus was a Roman god who was very important to the people of that time. His main function was to protect them from wolves. Wolves were a real, present danger at that age. These fierce, hungry animals roamed the vast forests which covered most of the land carrying off the farmers' sheep and goats. They were so bold in their attacks on farms that not even farmers and their families were safe from becoming the objects of their hunger. Their hearts certainly were not filled with love for humankind.

Each year during the middle of February, the Romans would hold a feast to honor their god, Lupercus, giving him thanks for helping protect them from the wolves. One legend actually credits the god with saving the city of Rome from many, dangerous packs of wolves. Grateful for this act of protection, the people held a festival in appreciation of Lupercus' actions on their behalf. Like all pagan festivals, this was a time of feasting and fun. The people would dance and play games. It was a fun time especially for unmarried men and women. A bowl would be placed in the center of the square. Girls would put their names in the bowl. Each young man would draw a name, and that girl would become his partner for the dance or game. Often these chance pairings evolved into sweetheart relationships.

This feast celebration went on for hundreds of years before the Christian religion came to Rome. As people like Valentine and others stood firm in their faith and died for their love of Christ, Christianity profoundly impacted the Roman way of life. Over time, the Romans and others began to discard their worship of many gods and embraced faith in Christ. Consequently, they no longer believed in the power of gods such as Lupercus. But Lupercalia was a happy time, and the people did not want to give it up. So they kept their holiday in the middle of February honoring Valentine who was said to have died in Rome on February 14. Other sources say that Valentine's birthday was actually February 14, the day before the old Roman celebration of honoring the "wolf destroyer." But whatever the reason for the selection of the date, the birth or death of Valentine, Christians now embraced February 14 as a day to say "I love you."

Verse 2 of "Love Divine, All Loves Excelling"

Reader 3 (*Wears a valentine with the letter* V *on it*): The celebration of Valentine's Day spread from Rome to France and England as the empire and its influence spread. Many of the ways of celebrating the day remained the same as the way it had been done in Rome over the years. Young men still chose their partners for games and dances by drawing a name from a bowl. When a man chose his sweetheart on Saint Valentine's Day, he called her his "valentine." The English actually believed that this was the day that the birds chose their mates, so that Valentine's Day was a good day for choosing one's future sweetheart. Geoffrey Chaucer, the famous fourteenth century English poet, wrote of the dream he had in "Parliament of Fowls" which solidified this belief in the hearts of the people. He stated: "For this was on Saint Valentine's Day, / When every bird cometh there to choose his mate."

So if it worked for birds, why not for humans? The heart needs a form of expressing its affection and love for another. Letters of love become that means. Sent on Saint Valentine's Day, these letters became known as "valentines." They began as a few words, "I give you my heart." Then pictures were added for a nice touch. Flowers and lace were added to make it beautiful. Cupids and hearts became associated with the cards. Gifts such as candy, cakes, flowers and jewels were given to show the valentine a heart filled with love.

The custom of caroling on this day was carried out by children in England hundreds of years ago. They would dress up as adults and go from house to house singing valentine songs like:

36

Good morning to you, valentine.
Curl your locks as I do mine —
Two before and three behind.
Good morning to you, valentine.

— "St. Valentine's Day," Clyde Robert Bulla,
   Thomas Crowell Co., NY, 1965

When the English colonized our nation, they brought with them the tradition of celebrating this special day. Today it has a special significance to hearts yearning to love. Once sweethearts gave valentines only to one another. Now the exchanging of valentines with others is big business. The card shops are filled with fancy, pink, red, and white cards, foiled envelopes, plain witty notes, eloquent verse rhymes and cartoon characters, large and small. All are meant to show our love as they are sent to friends, families, the boss, and neighbors. Children make valentines for parents in school. They create valentine boxes to hold the special cards they exchange. We will feast on those days with valentine cupcakes decorated with cinnamon hearts, cut-out heart cookies frosted with decorative glaze, boxes of delicious chocolates, or candy hearts. This is a night when men might not draw a name from a fish bowl for a partner to dine with, but one which usually sees many couples dining out. Long stemmed roses or red and pink carnations and helium balloons find their ways into the hands of special valentines. Gifts of jewels, stuffed animals, and after shave are exchanged.

Verse 3 "Love Divine, All Loves Excelling"

Reader 4 (*Wears a valentine with the letter* E *on it*): In some ways, the valentine parties and celebrations of today mirror the feasts on Lupercalia so long ago. For behind our celebration is the desire of the heart to express its love. This is what we really need to remember not only on this day but every day of our lives. God calls us to love him and to love one another with our whole hearts. God is love. His love was manifested for us in the greatest valentine gift of all, Jesus Christ. ''For God so loved the world, that he gave his only Son, so that everyone who believes in him may not perish, but have eternal life'' (John 3:16).

Jesus is God's heart given for the salvation of each one of us. But, like the unopened valentines collected by the students in school, that love cannot be known or experienced until the valentine envelope is unsealed and read. This is God's hope — that we will open the gift of salvation today. As we receive the Good News of God's love poured out for us in the death and resurrection of Jesus Christ, we realize how much we are loved as God's children. Those who receive that Good News and embrace that love then become messengers to others sending their special valentines of love in witness and action.

Go forth from this day in the knowledge that the roots of the celebration of this holiday, pagan as they were, go back even further for us as Christians. They have their origin in the very heart of God who loves us and reaches out to restore that broken relationship of sin through love and forgiveness. Rejoice that you are loved by one whose heart was filled to overflowing with love for his creation and his Son. Fill your heart with God's love, and share that love with all around. Happy Valentine's Day from all four of us and from our Lord and Savior, Jesus Christ! (*All four readers stand in line spelling L-O-V-E*) Amen.

Verse 4 of ''Love Divine, All Loves Excelling''

Games before or after the program

Game 1: *Things Associated With Valentine's Day*
1. pcdiu (cupid)
2. leetvanin drac (valentine card)
3. rmcaoen (romance)
4. tshaer (hearts)
5. skis (kiss)
6. ghu (hug)
7. ycdna (candy)
8. rsfelow (flowers)
9. cehooclsta (chocolates)
10. gaecros (corsage)
11. clae nda boribn (lace and ribbon)
12. a teda (a date)
13. velo (love)
14. gineb ghettoer (being together)
15. na veening tuo (an evening out)
16. a ndcalelgthi idnern (a candlelight dinner)
17. a ledciisou elam (a delicious meal)
18. a zodne sreos (a dozen roses)
19. het ocolr der (the color red)
20. wob nda orarw (bow and arrow)

Game 2: *A Valentine Examination*
   In groups of two or three share the following answers with each other.
1. Where did you first meet your Valentine date?
2. How long have you been sweethearts?
3. How long have you known each other?
4. What is special about Valentine's Day to you?
5. How often do you date your Valentine?
6. When you were courting, where were some of the places you would go? What were some of the things you enjoyed doing together? What do you do now?
7. What has been your most memorable date?
8. Do you send Valentine cards out? To whom?

9. Have you ever surprised your Valentine? How?
10. What's your favorite term of endearment for your loved one? His or hers for you?

Game 3: *A Valentine Race*

Write down a male and a female name to correspond with the letters listed below. You must have a different male and female name for each letter listed. First one done is our Valentine winner!

H	V	D
A	A	A
P	L	Y
P	E	
Y	N	
	T	
	I	
	N	
	E	
	S	

Example: H — Harry/Hilda

4

From Slavery To Sainthood!

Leader's Helps

"From Slavery To Sainthood!" is a program designed especially for remembering the Irish saint, Patrick. Participants journey as a leader and six readers tell the tale of this young boy sold into slavery and of his rising to become a recognized saint in the church.

Leader's parts are interspersed in the program.

Six readers hold signs connected to their talks:
Reader 1: Shamrock.
Reader 2: Map of Great Britain, with countries England, Scotland and Ireland marked.
Reader 3: Scroll with "Good News" across it and shamrock seal.
Reader 4: Snake with word "Legends" hung from neck.
Reader 5: Ball and chain with word "Slave" written on ball.
Reader 6: Large key with "Saint" written on it.

Songs include:
Opening hymn: "Rise Up, O Saints Of God"
Verses 1 and 2 of "I Love Your Kingdom, Lord"
Verses 3 and 4 of "I Love Your Kingdom, Lord"
Closing Hymn: "For All The Saints"

Decorations:
If a fellowship hour follows the program, decorate with green shamrocks and other appropriate Saint Patrick's Day items.

Program

A Program For Saint Patrick's Day

Opening Hymn: "Rise Up, O Saints Of God"

Leader: On March 17 Americans of Irish ancestry celebrate a special holiday known to us as Saint Patrick's Day. Schoolchildren and others of Irish descent make sure they sport the color green in one form or another on that day, declaring that they have some Irish blood flowing through their veins. Others join in the celebration as grand parades are held in the cities of Boston, Philadelphia, and New York. Clad in bright green, marchers troop down the avenues of these cities waving emerald flags which say "Erin go Bragh" (Ireland forever). Walking sticks, called shillelaghs, are carried by many who have made sure that their trousers, hats, coats, ties, and socks all coordinate with the Emerald Isle.

Reader 1 (*Holds up a green shamrock*): The color green is symbolic of Ireland's green and pleasant fields rich in shamrocks. Green beer flows from the taps in taverns this night while many take the opportunity to live it up. Centerpieces of green Irish hats and white clay pipes can be found decorating tables while florists dip white carnations in green. Home parties find games such as drawing the pig with your eyes closed and presenting a china pig bank as a prize, remembering Saint Patrick's days as a swineherd. Pipers play while Irish jigs and reels are danced. Old Irish tunes and songs flow over the airwaves and in restaurants. Three-leaf clovers are worn on many lapels. The shamrock has become the traditional symbol of Ireland based on the legend that Saint Patrick used it to explain the Trinity to those he was trying to convert.

Reader 2 (*Holds up a sign of Great Britain with the countries written on it*): Saint Patrick (389-461 A.D.), the patron saint of Ireland, is attributed with being chiefly responsible for the conversion of the people of that island to Christianity. Born in the area known today as Scotland, he lived in Britain during the days when the Roman Empire was abandoning the island to its fate and before the English nation appeared. His father was a wealthy alderman, who governed a territory as a viceroy or a ruling magistrate. Patrick's family was Christian and so the young boy was educated in the faith. However, at age 16 Patrick was captured by pirates who frequently raided the coastline of England. Sold into slavery in Ireland, the young boy served as a swineherd and tended sheep for an Irish chieftain in Ulster. During his captivity, Patrick dedicated himself to his religion. For six years, the boy worked as a slave, enduring much hardship compared to his former life. Finally, he was able to escape his captors and fled on a ship bound for Gaul (France), where he lived as a monk. Returning to Britain, he never forgot his experiences in pagan Ireland. He became driven with the idea of converting the Irish to Christianity. In a dream, Patrick heard the Irish calling, "We pray thee, holy youth, to come and walk amongst us as before." Patrick responded by preparing himself for his call. Returning to France, he studied at a monastery on an island off the southeast coast of France. From there he went to Auxerre, France, where he studied religion under Saint Germanus, a French bishop. After 14 years of study and preparation, he felt equipped to do the mission God was calling him to in Ireland. However, his superiors were reluctant to let him return because his earlier education was inadequate. But God's timing is always right, and when Palladius, the first missionary pope to Ireland, died in 431, Pope Celestine I sent Patrick with the title of bishop and his blessing. With love for God's kingdom and the Church of Jesus Christ overflowing in his heart, Patrick set off for Ireland to share the Good News.

Hymn: "I Love Your Kingdom, Lord" (Verses 1 and 2)

Leader: Known as the Apostle to the Irish, Patrick worked among the tribes in northern and western Ireland where no one had previously preached Christianity. Gaining the trust and friendship of several tribal leaders, he soon made many converts. During his ministry there, he founded 300 churches and baptized 120,000 people. Churches need pastors and Patrick looked to England and France for clergymen to serve them. However, the success he had in bringing people to Christ caused many of his superiors to take him to task for his ways in organizing the churches and his dedication to these inferior peoples. Patrick's letters reflected his resentment toward the scornful attitude of British clergymen and nobility toward the Irish.

Reader 3 (*Holds up scroll with "Good News" written across it and shamrock as seal*): We learn the most about Saint Patrick from his writings. A man of deep, spiritual development, he thanked God for the call to serve the Lord in Ireland. A humble servant of God, he dedicated himself to spreading the Good News across this island. Success was with him in spite of the opposition of his peers. In defense of his call, he wrote papers justifying his mission to the Irish people. Not afraid to speak out against those in power, he criticized a British chieftain for a raid on Ireland where several converts were killed.

Reader 4 (*Holds up snake with "Legends" written across it*): There are many legends which add spice to the life of Saint Patrick. The most famous is the story of how he charmed the snakes and toads of the island into the sea, where they drowned. Of course, the other is the use of the three-leaf shamrock in his education of the pagans to the triune God. It is believed that this legend is the basis for the shamrock as a traditional symbol of Ireland. Saint Patrick is also said to have been 120 years old when he died, and legend states that there was no night for 12 days after his death on March 17, 461. Truth or legend, it makes for an interesting tale of one who found great joy in sharing the Good News of Jesus.

Hymn: "I Love Your Kingdom, Lord" (Verses 3 and 4)

Leader: All we know of Saint Patrick's rise from slavery to sainthood makes the man whom this day celebrates an interesting study for us as Christians. His foundation of education in the faith and love of a Christian family stayed with him in his capacity. Proverbs 22:6 tells us to train our children in the way they should go, and they will not depart from it when they grow older. Taken from the love and support of his family and church, Patrick found himself, like Joseph, a slave living in a foreign land. It was during his time of slavery and imprisonment that Joseph, the young boy, grew to an even stronger faith in God. Patrick did also as he dedicated himself to trusting God to deliver him. God's Spirit continued to call to Patrick, as he did to the young boy Samuel, to serve him as a priest. Like Samuel who said, "Speak, Lord, your servant is listening," Patrick responded to a life dedicated solely to serving God among a people who had lost their sight, as Israel had during Eli's time. Like John the Baptist who was prepared by God for a powerful ministry, Patrick's time of study in the Word and prayer brought forth a great movement of the Spirit. The Spirit appeared to Saint Paul in a vision and called him to Macedonia to preach the Good News. The Spirit appeared to Saint Patrick in a vision and called him to Ireland to a people who had never heard the message of salvation.

Reader 5 (*Holds up sign of ball and chain with "Slave" written on it*): Patrick and Paul had been enslaved in their lives — Patrick as a real slave in bondage; Saul, later to be called Paul, a slave to the law. It was Christ who set them both free to follow the Spirit. Obedient to the call of God in their lives, these men chose to become slaves to the gospel so that others might have the freedom of salvation. Both men met with opposition to their ministries. Peter and James and the other leaders of the church struggled with Paul's mission to the Gentiles. Many went out to deliberately oppose him. Paul's struggles are recorded in the Book of Acts. Saint Patrick overcame the opposition of his fellow clergy through the advancement of the proclamation of the gospel as many were added to the family of God in spite of the "proper way" of evangelization.

Reader 6 (*Holds up a key with the word "Saint" written on it*): The message of Saint Patrick's Day to us is one of rising above the approval of humans and responding to the call of God to share with those who need to hear the message of salvation. We can all rise from slavery to sainthood as we die to our bondage to sin and are raised to new life in Christ; for God has chosen us to be members of his family, a chosen race, a royal priesthood — saints enslaved to their Lord and Master Jesus Christ. Jesus is the key which sets us free from sin. Jesus is the key to our salvation.

Leader: Go forth today remembering Saint Patrick and his love for Christ. Go forth covered not in green in honor of the Irish, but in red in remembrance of the precious blood of Jesus Christ shed for your salvation. Sing your hymns of praise and dance your jigs of joy! Swing your shillelaghs high as you walk in step with the Spirit. Rejoice as you march with all the saints sharing Christ's love and spreading the kingdom from shore to shore. May we all find rest with Saint Patrick and Saint Paul when our work for God and the Kingdom of Christ is done. Amen.

Closing Hymn: "For All The Saints"

5

Lenten Hopes

Leader's Helps

"Lenten Hopes: A Celebration of Lenten Disciplines" is a program designed especially for Lent. It may be used as a mid-week Lenten service, a women's program, a youth worship service, or a worship alternative on Sunday morning or evening.

This program involves a reflector and seven readers. The prayers are read by all the congregation gathered. After each prayer, a candle is lighted. Candles may be purple for the Lenten season and placed across the front of the audience. The hymns used reflect the Lenten topics and are taken from the *Lutheran Book Of Worship*.

The program is introduced with the celebration of Lent by the church. Topics covered by the meditations are fasting, special commitments, almsgiving, the study of the Word, prayer, and the cost of salvation. An offering and prayers may be added following the program if desired.

Program

A Celebration Of Lenten Disciplines

Opening Hymn: "O Lord, Throughout These Forty Days" (vv. 1, 4)

Lenten Meditation 1: The Celebration Of Lent

Reflector: On Ash Wednesday the Christian Church enters the season celebrated as Lent. Derived from the Middle English word "lente" meaning "spring time," Lent is a 40-day period of anticipation. Traditionally a time of repentance and renewal, the observance of Lent and its emphasis on penitential practices has evolved over the centuries. In the early church, candidates were prepared for Easter baptism during this time. Public penance for sins, once rigidly stressed, gradually gave way to a period of private penance. Christians took on Lenten obligations such as abstinence from meat and other foods and not attending festivities. The passage of time also saw these practices become less rigid with today's emphasis of Lent as a time for meditation and reflection on Easter's meaning.

For the Christian, the Easter celebration is enhanced by individual Lenten preparation. Through the exercise of Lenten disciplines, the Christian is made more aware of how Christ chose to give himself for us completely. Many outside the church and within see this as a gloomy time when pressure is brought to give up a favorite food or a comfortable habit or to attend worship more frequently. Christians should see this time as what it is meant to be: a time of celebration! Join us tonight as we journey, "celebrating" Lent by drawing closer to the one it centers on: Jesus Christ and his walk to Calvary and his glorious resurrection. May the words of the Apostle Paul guide us as we begin our celebration.

48

Reader: "Do you not know that all of us who have been baptized into Christ Jesus were baptized into his death? Therefore we have been buried with him by baptism into death, so that just as Christ was raised from the dead by the glory of the Father, so we too might walk in newness of life" (Romans 6:3-4). Let us pray.

All: Lord, as we enter this time of Lent, help us to celebrate the newness of life you offer the world. Bring springtime out of the winters of our discontented souls. Bring renewal out of our repentance. Breathe new freshness into our stale spirits, and help us to rejoice in the gift of eternal life obtained in Jesus Christ, your Son. In his name, Amen.

(Light Candle 1)

Hymn: "In The Hour Of Trial" (v. 1)

Lenten Meditation 2: The Discipline Of Fasting

Reader: The Scripture for our second Lenten meditation, The Discipline Of Fasting, is from 1 Corinthians 6:19. Saint Paul writes, "Do you not know that your body is a temple of the Holy Spirit within you, which you have from God?"

Reflector: When I think of Lent, I visualize a chocolate eclair, filled with gooey cream and topped with lots of thick icing. However, I do not indulge in many of these delicious confectioneries for I know what they will do to my caloric intake for the day. Many of us can handle giving up certain foods or drinks during the 40-day period of Lent. We enjoy the benefits accompanying that denial — the loss of a few pounds. However, we need to examine the spiritual benefit of this practice that many participate in.

Lenten fasting takes on special meaning for Christians as they cleanse the body, mind, and soul. Fasting imposes self-discipline which many of us lack. It encourages meditation and reflection. The discipline of fasting takes on a variety of forms. It could be giving up one big meal a week and donating the money to world hunger or a favorite charity. It might mean choosing simpler, more healthy meals. Some people abstain from a favorite food or drink (meat, wine, desserts, and so forth). Others eliminate wasteful habits and expensive excesses. Saint Paul reminds us in our second reading that we are "temples" of God's Spirit. We are to glorify God with our bodies. However, we also need to have the right attitude when we fast so it does not become a salvation work. It is through God's grace that we are saved, not our works. The real benefit in Lenten fasting is that it helps us to recall Christ's suffering and his death to redeem humanity. Faith in Jesus, not our self-denial, should be our focus. We can boast about being able to abstain from between-meal snacks or sweets, but Christ's work upon the cross is his alone to be glorified.

This Lent practice fasting with the right attitude. We should think of ourselves as that chocolate eclair being emptied of that creamy filling. As an empty vessel, God can then fill us with more and more of his Spirit so that we can truly glorify God with our bodies and fasting. Let us pray.

All: Lord, we ask you to help us this Lent to focus in on you and not on our works. Help us to remember to boast only in you and what you have done and are doing in our lives. We praise you for the gift of self-discipline in our Lenten practices. Help us to be true temples for your Holy Spirit who lives in us. Through Christ we pray, Amen.

(*Light Candle 2*)

Hymn: "Take My Life, That I May Be" (vv. 1, 5)

Lenten Meditation 3: Special Commitments

Reader: As an introduction to our third Lenten meditation on Special Commitments, I read from Psalm 37:5, "Commit your way to the Lord; trust in him and he will act."

50

Reflector: Have you browsed around the local book store lately? The next time you are in the mall, notice how many books there are in the self-improvement section. Our society is committed to improving itself and has directed us to channeling our energies in a variety of ways, all involving commitment of one sort or another. Lent is a time of special commitments that involve giving up or taking on something for a greater good. It is a time for improving the self according to the direction God moves the heart of the individual. Special Lenten commitments can be very positive acts with long-reaching benefits.

The psalmist in our reading exhorts the believer to commit one's way to the Lord. This is an intentional, positive act which benefits not only the individual, but others. It calls us to make deliberate choices in our walk of faith. In the area of discipline, it may call us to watch less television and read our Bible more. It may cause us to pass by McDonald's and place the money we save into a jar labeled "World Hunger." It may call us to attend mid-week Lenten worship with our family instead of staying at home vegetating because we are just burned out. Lent presents the opportunity to make such commitments. These may come through the church or outside of it. Visiting a shut-in neighbor or a nursing home resident is a commitment of time and energy, but the blessings are two-fold. Inviting a friend who rarely gets out of the house to lunch witnesses to the love and fellowship Christ calls us to share with others. When we commit our acts to the Lord, God does bless them and us. Take time to make this a practice, consecrating all you do to God. Be available for God. Be intentional about your actions. Your commitment to Christ will impact others. Intentional, positive acts done under the direction of the Holy Spirit affect both the giver and the recipient. Trust in God to direct and follow through in your commitments. Let God do the improving in your heart as the Lord channels you in the direction the Spirit chooses. Let us pray.

All: Dear Lord, we commit our ways unto you. Help us reach out beyond ourselves and trust in you to be with us. May the commitments we make in our Lenten journey bring renewal to our spirits and benefit others. We trust in you and delight in this hope. In Jesus' name, Amen.

(*Light Candle 3*)

Hymn: "We Give Thee But Thine Own" (v. 1)

Lenten Meditation 4: Almsgiving

Reader: As an introduction to our fourth meditation on Almsgiving, we read from Luke 21:1-2: "He looked up and saw rich people putting their gifts into the treasury; he also saw a poor widow put in two small copper coins."

Reflector: "Almsgiving" is a strange word to us today. Old Testament readings do not mention this practice of the duty of giving to the poor. This practice came about as the number of extremely poor people rose in Jesus' time. Over the centuries, this practice has certainly changed. Today we have a welfare system run by the government and not the church. Yet we do give to help others as we pass our collection plate at worship, turning our envelopes up so all will see or down so no one will know.

Giving in Christ's time was not the private affair of today's time. In fact, then great displays could be made if one wanted to flaunt one's giving before others. Placed in the Temple were horns which received the coins of the giver. Those wishing to make a public display of their stewardship tossed their money in with great zeal, causing the trumpets to echo with the clanging of their "tithe." Yet we see in our reading a stark contrast between two givers. One gives with pride while the other gives discreetly, quietly placing her two small coins into the treasury. A third party, however, observes this action. Jesus looks upon the scene. The rich should have been practicing the principle of almsgiving by presenting their offering not to the treasury but to the widow in their presence. Her need must have been obvious in comparison to their abundance. Yet they did not have eyes to see. Christ calls us to see that it is not the amount given to God that counts, but the attitude in which the offering is made. The rich gave out of their abundance and were proud of their contributions. The widow, whom they should have been helping, gave out of her poverty and put in all she had. Hers was a true offering; theirs a donation.

As we make special offerings this Lent, let us make sure that we give with Christian charity and with thanksgiving to the one who provides for us in all areas of our lives. Let our giving be truly an offering and not simply a donation. Let us pray.

All: Lord Jesus, we are reminded today that you see our motive in giving. Help us to give from hearts filled with love for you and for the mission and support of your Church. Help us to be aware of the needs around us. Remind us that all we have comes from you, and you give so that we can give to others. With grateful hearts we pray, Amen.

(*Light Candle 4*)

Hymn: "Lord, Keep Us Steadfast In Your Word" (v. 1)

Lenten Meditation 5: The Word Of God

Reader: As preparation for our meditation on the Word of God, we read from Deuteronomy 11:18: "You shall put these words of mine in your heart and soul; and you shall bind them as a sign on your hand, and fix them as an emblem on your forehead."

Reflector: Remember the charm bracelets of the early '60s? You could tell the approach of a teenage girl from the jingling of her wrist a block away. This fad prompted the buying of charms for the variety of interests one might have — a flute for music, a painting easel for art, a heart for a special friend, a graduation cap for that special day, and so forth. The charms reflected the personality and involvement of the wearer.

Our fifth reading talks of another symbol which we, as Christians, should be wearing, not only on the outside but on the inside as well. That symbol reflects the importance of the study of God's Holy Word. Many of us are proud of our knowledge in certain areas. Our home libraries boast many books which reflect our areas of interest. We collect certificates and diplomas in different areas of training. However, many of us struggle with our area of expertise in the Scriptures. Israel was commanded to lay up God's law in their hearts and souls. The Word of God was to permeate their entire being and culture. Their actions were to reflect and correspond to their study. As Christians, most of us need to repent of our lack of enthusiasm and discipline in our area of study. Lent gives us the opportunity to make a commitment to reading the holy book. In exercising this practice, we will grow in our understanding of the Bible and our Christian faith. We will then be able to incorporate that understanding into our daily lives by the inspiration of the living Word. We cannot unlock the messages of the Word with our limited human wisdom. But as we study and pray for understanding, God's Spirit will give us eyes to see and help us to understand. Begin today to set time aside for daily reading and reflection on the Word. Study the Word so you can wear the symbol of one growing in the knowledge of God. Let us pray.

All: Lord God, thank you that you continue to bless us when we do as you command. Help us in our study of your Word to come to a deeper understanding of Jesus Christ as our Lord and Savior. Help us to live out our faith in love and action. To you we pray, Amen.

(*Light Candle 5*)

Hymn: "Go To Dark Gethsemane" (v. 1)

Lenten Meditation 6: Prayer

Reader: Saint Paul tells us in Philippians 4:6, "Do not worry about anything, but in everything by prayer and supplication with thanksgiving let your requests be known to God." Let us remember that passage as we hear about prayer.

Reflector: "Anxiety!" The mere mention of that word makes our stress level rise. We are a nation preoccupied with the word and all it entails. We are anxious about our appearance. Am I wearing the correct thing? We are anxious about our children's grades. Will they get accepted into the National Honor Society or the college of their choice? We are anxious about our health. Am I eating the right foods? Drinking enough water? Will our government adopt a health care plan that will benefit me? The list goes on and on. Anxiety produces stress which erodes the foundation of our trust in our self-esteem, our educational system, the medical profession, the government, and so forth. Yet when we trust in anything besides God, we open ourselves up to being let down and becoming discouraged.

Saint Paul had a right to be discouraged as he wrote his letter to the church at Philippi to encourage them. Yet he sat in prison and rejoiced, not abandoning his hope in God or in the power of prayer. We must not become discouraged with the discipline of prayer. God sometimes allows us to feel dry and empty so that he can remind us that it is not our power that wrestles answers from the stronghold of heaven. We are called to relax and allow God's Spirit to pray. Picture a child climbing into a parent's lap to listen to a bedtime story. That is how God wants us to approach him in prayer. Anticipating an intimacy. Having ears open to hear what he has to say. Relaxing, secure in the knowledge that we are loved. Thankful for all God has done and is doing. Some of us feel limited in our prayer lives. Rejoice! God knows our limitations — even our inability at times to pray.

This Lent begin to be more intentional about making time to pray. Jesus spent nights in prayer. He drew apart from his demanding schedule to intercede for others but above all to be strengthened for the day ahead. He could have offered up many excuses, but he made the time and closeted himself with God. This Lent increase your time with God in prayer. Remember, however, that prayer is a two-way communication. We need time to listen as well as to speak. Focus in on the one you are praying to, using a lighted candle or a picture or an image. Then allow God to flood you with his peace. Let all anxiety disappear as God's presence brings you that blessed assurance of one who has heard. Let us pray.

All: Lord, we place all anxiety into your loving hands. Open our ears and enable us to be still. Help us to listen to what you have to say to us this Lent. With thankful hearts we come to you in prayer. Amen.

(*Light Candle 6*)

Hymn: "All Glory, Laud, And Honor" (vv. 1, 4)

Lenten Meditation 7: No Pain, No Gain

Reader: For our final reading we remember Jesus' approach into Jerusalem just before he was crucified. Hear what the prophet Zechariah has to say, "Lo, your king comes to you; triumphant and victorious is he, humble and riding on a donkey, on a colt, the foal of a donkey" (Zechariah 9:9). Now hear our final reflection, No Pain, No Gain, and recall what it cost God to sacrifice his beloved Son.

Reflector: Have you ever been given the opportunity to be humbled? Most of us would like to forget about those times when that uncomfortable experience has been offered to us. Just when we are thinking of ourselves as persons of importance, something happens to bring a bit of embarrassment into our lives. Then we slide down to the bottom of the ladder when we felt so secure at the top. At times our overinflated views of who we are and what we can do crash into the reality of events in our lives and make us feel very humble.

In our final reading we see a king. This king did not ride the prancing white steed of a conqueror, but a donkey, an animal of burden. Jesus entered Jerusalem in this humble manner to declare his kingship over a world and people who have an overinflated idea of who they are. As Christians we take the opportunity as we begin Holy Week to walk our Lord's final steps on earth. We travel from Palm Sunday's glory, laud, and honor to the Last Supper on Maundy Thursday where Christ establishes a new covenant, a memorial of his suffering and death observed in the sacrament of his body and blood. We go to the Garden of Gethsemane and see Christ's passion. We enter the darkness of Good Friday without which there is no Easter Sunday. We cannot reach the glorified Christ of Easter without experiencing the pain of the Cross of Calvary.

Growth in our lives often is accompanied by pain. For Christians, the one who suffered the pain of our sins is Jesus. Jesus knew no sin yet became sin so that we could have eternal life. Without embracing Christ's pain, we stand in judgment for our individual sins. By recognizing his sacrifice and accepting him as Savior, we are reconciled to God. Jesus' pain was real, and the gain is ours to accept or reject. Salvation is a free gift, but one to be appropriated in our lives. The pain was his; the gain is ours. The choice is yours. Make a commitment as you approach the final week of Lent to travel the steps Jesus took through quiet reflection. Ask yourself where you stand in your personal relationship with Jesus. Journey to the cross and receive God's grace. Rise to new life with the Resurrected Lord. Rejoice, for your king has come offering you the gift of humility and love! Celebrate that gift as your climax to the Lenten journey. Let us pray.

All: Lord Jesus, we repent of the condition of our souls. Forgive us for being proud and not acknowledging your lordship in our lives. Fill us with new insight to the depth of your passion and our need for forgiveness. Thank you for the pain that has become our gain. In your holy name we pray. Amen.

Benediction

Leader: Now may the blessing of God the Father, the Son, and the Holy Spirit go with you as you journey throughout the rest of this Lenten season.

All: We celebrate Lent and our Lord Jesus Christ. Amen.

Closing Hymn: "Were You There When They Crucified My Lord?" (vv. 1-4)

Bulletin

Lenten Hopes

Opening Hymn: "O Lord, Throughout These Forty Days" (vv. 1, 4)

Lenten Meditation 1: The Celebration Of Lent

Reflector

Reader

Prayer
All: Lord, as we enter this time of Lent, help us to celebrate the newness of life you offer the world. Bring springtime out of the winters of our discontented souls. Bring renewal out of our repentance. Breathe new freshness into our stale spirits, and help us to rejoice in the gift of eternal life obtained in Jesus Christ, your Son. In his name, Amen.

(Light Candle 1)

Hymn: "In The Hour Of Trial" (v. 1)

Lenten Meditation 2: The Discipline Of Fasting

Reader

Reflector

Prayer
All: Lord, we ask you to help us this Lent to focus in on you and not our works. Help us to remember to boast only in you and what you have done and are doing in our lives. We praise you for the gift of self-discipline in our Lenten practices. Help us to be true temples for your Holy Spirit who lives in us. Through Christ we pray, Amen.

(*Light Candle 2*)

Hymn: "Take My Life, That I May Be" (v. 1)

Lenten Meditation 3: Special Commitments

Reader

Reflector

Prayer
All: Dear Lord, we commit our ways unto you. Help us reach out beyond ourselves and trust in you to be with us. May the commitments we make in our Lenten journey bring renewal to our spirits and benefit others. We trust in you and delight in this hope. In Jesus' name, Amen.

(*Light Candle 3*)

Hymn: "We Give Thee But Thine Own" (v. 1)

Lenten Meditation 4: Almsgiving

Reader

Reflector

Prayer
All: Lord Jesus, we are reminded today that you see our motive in giving. Help us to give from hearts filled with love for you and for the mission and support of your Church. Help us to be aware of the needs around us. Remind us that all we have comes from you, and you give so that we can give to others. With grateful hearts we pray, Amen.

(*Light Candle 4*)

Hymn: "Lord, Keep Us Steadfast In Your Word" (v. 1)

Lenten Meditation 5: The Word Of God

Reader

Reflector

Prayer
All: Lord God, thank you that you continue to bless us when we do as you command. Help us in our study of your Word to come to a deeper understanding of Jesus Christ as our Lord and Savior. Help us to live out our faith in love and action. To you we pray, Amen.

(*Light Candle 5*)

Hymn: "Go To Dark Gethsemane" (v. 1)

Lenten Meditation 6: Prayer

Reader

Reflector

Prayer
All: Lord, we place all anxiety into your loving hands. Open our ears and enable us to be still. Help us to listen to what you have to say to us this Lent. With thankful hearts we come to you in prayer. Amen.

(*Light Candle 6*)

Hymn: "All Glory, Laud, And Honor" (vv. 1, 4)

Lenten Meditation 7: No Pain, No Gain

Reader

Reflector

Prayer

All: Lord Jesus, we repent of the condition of our souls. Forgive us for being proud and not acknowledging your lordship in our lives. Fill us with new insight to the depth of your passion and our need for forgiveness. Thank you for the pain that has become our gain. In your holy name we pray, Amen.

Benediction

Leader: Now may the blessing of God the Father, the Son, and the Holy Spirit go with you as you journey throughout the rest of this Lenten season.

All: We celebrate Lent and our Lord Jesus Christ. Amen.

Closing Hymn: "Were You There When They Crucified My Lord?" (vv. 1-4)

*Optional
   Offering/Offertory
   Prayers of the Church
   Dismissal hymn

6

Women Blessing Through Marriage

Leader's Helps

"Women Blessing Through Marriage" gives women in the congregation an opportunity to recall their wedding days. This program is ideal for a Mother/Daughter celebration, a summer event, or a kick-off program in the fall. A fellowship meal may precede the event or follow. Decorations for fellowship can be bells, crepe paper, and so forth. A wedding cake may be served as dessert. Photo albums, wedding pictures, and other memorabilia may be placed to view. Special prizes may be given for the person married the longest and the person most recently married. Questions to be shared over a meal might be: Where were you married? Did you have a honeymoon? What was unique about your wedding day? If you had one thing to do over, what would it be? Participants should have a write-up on their gown, their marriage date, those involved in the wedding, and other interesting facts concerning that celebration. As the women model their gowns, the leader will read that write-up. If available, flower girls or bridesmaids may be included. This gives youth opportunity to share in the event as well.

Music: Opening hymn — "Blessed Be The Tie That Binds"
Closing hymn: "Joyful, Joyful, We Adore Thee"

A pianist should play some appropriate numbers while the models walk to the front of the sanctuary. Have all brides come back for a final viewing. Special music in the form of a solo or ensemble may be used to break up the line of models and add variety to the program.

Bulletin

Our Brides And Their Special Day

Leader

Reading: 1 Corinthians 13:1-13

Leader

Opening Hymn: "Blessed Be The Tie That Binds"

List name of each bride, date of marriage, and model's name if gown is being worn by another. Give description of each model's gown and some background information on her wedding day. Have participants put something of special interest in their accounts. Leader will then read these in order.

Special Music

List names of remaining brides (and information as above).

Leader

Reading: Ephesians 5:25-33

Leader

Closing Hymn: "Joyful, Joyful, We Adore Thee"

Program

Leader: Jesus celebrated marriage at the wedding feast of Cana. For centuries men and women have been blessed through this union of two becoming one. The writer of Ecclesiastes tells us: "Two are better than one, because they have a good reward for their toil. For if they fall, one will lift up the other; but woe to the one who is alone and falls and does not have another to help. Again, if two lie together, they keep warm; but how can one keep warm alone? And though one might prevail against another, two will withstand one. A threefold cord is not quickly broken" (Ecclesiastes 4:9-12).

The blessing of marriage is that we are united to another to walk this life by faith. With Christ as our third party, all things are possible. Tonight we remember that bond and celebrate the Word proclaimed in love and recall the blessing of the day our participants were wed. Hear from 1 Corinthians 13 concerning love.

Reading: 1 Corinthians 13:1-13.

Leader: The gift of love is a blessing. This passage is often read at wedding ceremonies along with the passage on love from Ruth. Ruth here declares her love for her mother-in-law, a love that goes beyond the physical, and a love which we all desire to incorporate in our lives.

Reading: Ruth 1:16-17

Leader: As we begin our special bridal show, let us join our hearts by singing "Blessed Be The Tie That Binds."

Our Brides And Their Special Day: Leader reads information about each bride and gown and her wedding day as each participant models her dress.

Special Music: Solo or other special performance

Leader reads information about remaining participants as each models her gown. Following the last model, the program concludes with the following statement.

Leader: For centuries women have blessed men and children in marriage. The love we give to others comes back upon us a thousandfold. However, sometimes that love is rejected and God's heart is pained as ours are. But Saint Paul tells us in Colossians that we are to bear with each other and forgive whatever grievances we may have against one another. Sometimes the blessing of marriage is robbed from us through circumstances beyond our control. Yet in Ephesians Paul calls for husbands to love their wives as Christ loved the church. Hear our final reading.

Reading: Ephesians 5:25-33

Leader: May Jesus Christ, who has blessed us in this life, continue to bring joy to our marriages and to us as his brides. May you present yourselves before your groom, Jesus Christ, pure and spotless in your wedding gown of faith. Let us join our hearts and voices once more in "Joyful, Joyful, We Adore Thee."

Thanks should be extended to the hostess committee and program committee and to all who shared their gowns, albums, and decorations.

7

A Humorous Look At Some Hopeful Women

Leader's Helps

This resource, "A Humorous Look At Some Hopeful Women," is an excellent program for a Mother/Daughter banquet, a fall kick-off salad supper and program, or any other time of the year when your group gathers together. It is not limited to just a women's organization program event as it explores the hopes six women have in God.

Participants include:

Narrator: Introduces and concludes the program. May assist with leading the singing of the various chorus verses.

Eve: This woman can dress accordingly (flesh tights and leotard with three green leaves attached to strategic spots) and carry a basket of apples.

Mrs. Noah: This reader dresses as the patriarch Noah's wife and carries an umbrella.

Sarah: This woman can be an older lady of the congregation. She should put a pillow under her robe to give the appearance of being very pregnant. You may use a pregnant woman in your congregation also.

Paul's Mother: Dresses as a Hebrew of that day and carries a feathered pen and scroll.

Lydia: Dresses in purple robe and carries letters.

Dorcas: Carries sewing basket and quilt.

Songs:
"Don't Sit Under The Apple Tree"
"Row, Row, Row Your Boat"
"Sailing, Sailing"

"Rock-a-bye, Baby"
"Mother"
"I'm Gonna Sit Right Down And Write Myself A Letter"
"My Blue Heaven"
"It's A Long Way To Tipperary"
"Quilting Party"
"Row, Row, Row Your Boat"

All of the above songs should be in the realm of public domain. The words have been adapted to the situation.

Song sheet included at the end of program.

Program

Narrator: Flash! We interrupt your regularly scheduled program for tonight with this announcement: A great, new discovery of ancient writers from Bible times has just been uncovered. Parts of an exciting manuscript have just been discovered sealed up in a 2,000-year-old mayonnaise jar at the bottom of a basket of ironing. Our researchers have concluded that the basket belonged to Saint Spray N. Wash, a devoted, Christian mother. Now Spray was in a hurry the day all manuscripts were to be handed in to the chairperson of the committee that compiled the Bible for publication. It had been one of those days we all have. Her oldest son needed a lift to the harp and lyre factory; her youngest had oratory practice at the forum; and her new chariot lost a wheel. No lemon laws back then, but I'm sure we can all relate to her reason for missing the deadline. So she just stuck the paper in a jar to return to the chairperson, but she got sidetracked hauling up her ironing to the second floor of her home and never quite got around to handing it in. Because of the age of the paper, translators have only been able to decipher fragments of this lost publication which gives new insight into the lives of some rather well-known biblical women. And so, this evening you are in for a treat as our program committee of Prime Time Talented Players presents a new look at some special women. Join me now in our first chorus of introduction.

Chorus: ''Don't Sit Under The Apple Tree''
Don't sit under the apple tree with anyone else but me, anyone else but me, anyone else but me. No! No! No! Just remember that I've been true to nobody else but you ... so just be true to me.

Eve (*Carries basket of apples*): Boy, did I goof! I never should have listened to that snaky reptile. Did he ever give me a line! God told Adam and me explicitly that we couldn't eat of the fruit from the tree that was planted smack dab in the middle of his garden. But you know how it is when something is forbidden! It becomes all the more enticing. I should have listened to God. I realize in hindsight that he always wants my best, but that crafty serpent spun quite a temptation for me. He enticed me with promises of gaining vast knowledge. Looking into the future he showed me beautiful clothes of silks and spandex. Now running around naked gives one a sense of freedom, but the thought of draping myself in luxury was very enticing, not to mention showing off my figure with that tight-fitting stuff. The vision of little white ermine around my neck instead of scurrying over my feet took hold of me. Then that picture of a grand castle located by a lake with hanging gardens. That sure beat living under those trees and sleeping on the ground. Campers can relate to all that dropping pitch and morning dew. That comfortable king-size bed looked very inviting. What dreams he spun for me. The world painted by his sweet tongue sounded so grand . . . so grand . . . just one, small bite . . . that's all I took. Want my apple? I have a lot here in my basket. Take a bite . . . it won't hurt. Just one small bite . . . Oh, my . . . what a mistake that was. (*Sighs*) I didn't realize what a dream life I had till it was all snatched from me, but you know the end of that story. But don't let me rain on your party. Just go on with your singing. It looks like quite a storm headed our way. (*Sits down*)

Chorus: "Row, Row, Row Your Boat"
Noah's wife, Noah's wife, dreams of life ashore. All the animals on the ark become a smelly bore. Rainy days, stormy days, 'mid the birds and beasts. She cooks, she cleans, but work's never done on that stinking, floating zoo!

Mrs. Noah (*Carries an unopened umbrella*): Now ladies, we women ask little of life. Right? So when a special occasion arises, we have a right to celebrate with a little style. That's how I felt when I wanted to celebrate my 500th wedding anniversary. "Let's go on a cruise, Noah," I announced over supper. We weren't getting any younger. We just celebrated 600 years on this earth. "How much longer, Noah, do you expect to live?" I asked him. "Let's have fun while we're still able to enjoy it. You know — make hay while the sun shines." That's not too much to ask, is it? Now I was thinking of one of those nice Carnival cruises — you know, the kind where you don't have to cook or clean or take care of those 3 boys of ours. Maybe we could play a little deck tennis or shuffleboard — swim in the pool — get a little tan — listen to the music of Methuselah and his Merry Music Makers. A simple cruise but with lots of fringe benefits. Sound romantic? Well, I need to be put into a better mood to tell you how it all turned out. So help me out and sing our next chorus.

Chorus: "Sailing, Sailing"
Sailing, sailing, over the bounding main ... (*continue humming softly*).

Mrs. Noah: I never expected that man to go overboard, but listen to what happened to my dream vacation. It all began with Noah trying to save a little money by building this huge ark, right in our back yard. The neighbors had a field day, but Noah insisted God told him to build this boat. Why didn't he move us to the seaside then so everyone would stop laughing? Job transfers were very easy in our time. It was a mobile society. At least on the seaside we'd have water for that monstrous ark. But no, he had to build it on dry land — hundreds of miles from the nearest port. Yep, 600 years had taken their toll on the old guy's mind. Then when he was done, he just came and told me to gather up everything I wanted and climb on board. No chance to go out and buy some new duds for this cruise. And we weren't going alone. The boys and their wives were to come also. Not only that but he insisted on all those crazy animals — I mean this was going to be quite a carnival — a zoo — and also lots of work. I didn't see any porters or maids climbing on board. Just us! The idea of being cooped up with family and two of each kind of animal was more than I could bear, and I let him hear about it. Then he began to forecast rain, and there wasn't a cloud in the sky! Now ladies, I'm sure you all have treaded water with someone in life. But this looked like it was going to be like one of those trips you take where you go and pray there's a service station somewhere that you can stop at to ask questions "after" your hubby gets lost. Can you relate? Oh, my . . . it feels like there's a wind coming up. I'd better get on board. What was that I just felt? A raindrop? (*Opens umbrella*) Noah said to be prepared. Okay, so I listened. Just get back to your singing. Anyway, it's time for me to tend to rocking those babies to sleep. And you know, we wound up with plenty of them.

Chorus: "Rock-a-bye, Baby"
Rock-a-bye, baby, on the tree top. When the wind blows, the cradle will rock. When the bough breaks, the cradle will fall and down will come baby, cradle and all.

Sarah (*Very pregnant*): Just look at me. Mother would have a fit. I can just hear her now. "Sarah, no one has a baby at 90 years old. What will people think?" I can't believe this is happening to me! Me — pregnant at age 90. Of course I get all the tsk-tsks while 99-year-old Abraham gets pats on the back! Why didn't God make him the father of nations when I was younger? I heard that promise, too, but when it didn't happen I thought I'd help the situation by giving my slave girl, Hagar, to the old guy to bear me a child. Well, it worked out. Hagar had a baby boy and named him Ishmael because the Lord had heard her misery. But that mess only made all of us miserable. Then those three strangers came and told my husband that I would have a son in a year. Oh, how I laughed. Me — pregnant at my old age. People our age don't have babies. But here I am, girls, my belly swelling and sick every morning. The laugh is on me. (*Pats stomach*) God is so good . . . he does keep his promises. Sing a little for me, okay? This really is incredible. I'm going to be a mother.

Chorus: "Mother"

    M is for the million things God gives us
    O means only that we all will soon grow old
    T is for the tears that were shed to save me
    H is for Christ's heart of purest gold
    E is for God's eyes with love light shining
    R means right and right Christ'll always be
    Put them all together they spell MOTHER, a word
    that means God's love to me.

Paul's Mother (*Carries feather pen and scroll*): Mothers — they are fine people. They deserve a little respect from their children. Right? Well, thank God for Priscilla! If she didn't write me a letter once in a while, I'd never know where that son of mine was. Saul — remember me? I'm the one who bore you and washed your dirty face. I'm sure all of you out there understand. You go to all the effort and trouble of teaching a boy a trade, sacrificing to buy him a nice little tent shop and creating a good clientele. Then he goes off to rabbi school — but we understand those second career folk. Why didn't he settle down, find a nice Jewish girl, and give me some grandchildren? No, he gets mixed up with this religious stuff and becomes fanatical about it. The next thing we know he's off hunting down those Christians. Then, horror of horrors, I get news from friends in Damascus that he's lost his sight. Then he's seeing again and promoting this Christian thing. Even changes his name to Paul. I guess I'll never understand that boy. If only he'd write. He writes everyone else — people in Corinth, Ephesus, Rome, and Philippi — gives them lots of advice, I hear. But will he take some from me? Says he has things from God to share with them. Well, I wish God would tell him to write a letter to his mother. What's a mother to do? How about singing me some advice, ladies?

Chorus: "I'm Gonna Sit Right Down And Write Myself A Letter"

She's gonna sit right down and write herself a letter, and make believe it came from Paul. She's gonna write words, oh so nice; she's gonna read them once or twice. A lot of news will be inside. She'll be filled with pride.

She's gonna smile and say, "I hope you're feeling better," and close with love like good sons often do. She's gonna sit right down and write herself a letter and make believe it came from Paul.

Lydia (*Dresses in purple robe and carries letters*): Oh, heavens. What's that song I hear this evening? Sing it loud and clear. I need a little heaven on earth.

Chorus: "My Blue Heaven"

When whippoorwill calls and evening is nigh, I hurry to my purple heaven. A turn to the right, a little white light, will lead you to my purple heaven.

Lydia: Like my purple clothes, girls? Well, I don't. I'm up to my ears in purple. My shop is full of purple — Lydia's Purple Boutique where purple is the rage. Purple, purple, purple — all over the place. Do you know why? Purple is the cheapest dye I can buy. And as a shopkeeper, I have to make a profit to survive. Oh, by the way, the mail just came. Let's check the orders. Look here . . . a letter from Paul. I do wish he'd write his mother. Hmm . . . I remember that first day I heard Paul talk of Jesus. It was the Sabbath, and I had invited Paul and Timothy to be guests at my home. They couldn't get over all the purple — in fact, they commented on the "blinding" effect it had on them and chuckled. But that was the day they made it perfectly clear to me that Jesus was God's Son, the Messiah! What a privilege it was to make a home for those two faithful servants of God . . . even if it was just a

74

temporary place. How I yearned for orange, or yellow, or even bright green to decorate with, but those two were content with all my purple decor. You see they had learned to be content in all their circumstances — something I need to learn. (*Looks around*) Yes, I need to be grateful — even for purple. Well, I guess just confessing that has shown me that I have come a long way ... Yes, thanks to Jesus, I have definitely come a long way. Let me hear some traveling music for my continued journey, ladies.

Chorus: "It's A Long Way To Tipperary"
There's a home in Thyatria, far across the River Mazitza. Near the plains of Philippi, where purple is the dye. There lives Lydia and her servants who are anything but shy. There's a home in Thyatria, where purple is the dye.

Dorcas (*Carries sewing basket and quilt*): Come on in. Everyone, come in, and find a place to sit down. Yes, this is the spot ... Dorcas' place. How many do we have with us today? One, two, three, four, five, wow ... what a great turnout. How wonderful! We need all your helping hands to sew for the poor people of Joppa. Look, I'm working on some quilts for the children of the widow of fisherman John. Lydia sent down a bunch of purple fabric with a letter from Paul. He really should write his mother, you know. Where is Willy? Isn't she coming today? Is she sick? Willy always comes to sew. She's the one who got this group together. What's the matter with her today? I know she wanted to invite Susanna, Simon's wife. Now I know some of you think he is unclean because he's a tanner. But remember how Jesus healed the leper? There is no one more unclean than a leper. So maybe we ought to remember Jesus welcomes all people. Isn't that what you're saying about her, Miriam, that we should welcome her? Oh, good, here's Willy and Susanna. Come in, girls. We've all been waiting for you. Right, ladies? Let's start our quilting party by singing a little song.

Chorus: "Quilting Party"
> In the sky the bright stars glitter. On the bank the
> pale moon shines. It is in the city of Joppa that we
> are sewing purple quilts. We are sewing purple quilts,
> we are sewing purple quilts. It is in the home of Dor-
> cas that we are sewing purple quilts.

Chorus: "Row, Row, Row Your Boat"
> Sew, sew, sew your seams in a nice straight line;
> Sewing, sewing, sewing, sewing takes up all my time!

Narrator: Now hasn't this been an enlightening night? But
we've come to the end of our translation of our ancient writings. And it's just been reported that the rest of the manuscript
has been found in a baggie under a pile of socks waiting to
be darned, tucked into a volume of "How To Get A Chain
Letter Going To Mothers Who Feel The Need To Stay In Contact With Lost Sons," but that's another program. We do hope
you found this presentation entertaining and maybe even a little
educational. Good night, ladies ... maybe you could drop a
line to Paul and remind him to write his mom.
Ta-ta.

Adapted from a skit, "Humorous View of Some of the Bible Women,"
co-authored by the Northeastern Minnesota Synodical Women's Organization and the Southwestern Minnesota Synodical Women's Organization of
the Women of the ELCA and used by permission.

Song Sheet

A Humorous Look At Some Hopeful Women

Narrator

Chorus: "Don't Sit Under The Apple Tree"
Don't sit under the apple tree with anyone else but me, anyone else but me, anyone else but me. No! No! No! Just remember that I've been true to nobody else but you ... so just be true to me.

Eve

Chorus: "Row, Row, Row Your Boat"
Noah's wife, Noah's wife, dreams of life ashore. All the animals on the ark become a smelly bore. Rainy days, stormy days, 'mid the birds and beasts. She cooks, she cleans, but work's never done on that sinking floating zoo!

Mrs. Noah

Chorus: "Sailing, Sailing"
Sailing, sailing, over the bounding main ... (continue humming softly)

Mrs. Noah

Chorus: "Rock-a-bye, Baby"
Rock-a-bye, baby, on the tree top. When the wind blows, the cradle will rock. When the bough breaks, the cradle will fall and down will come baby, cradle and all.

Sarah

Chorus: "Mother"
M is for the million things God gives us
O means only that we all will soon grow old
T is for the tears that were shed to save me
H is for Christ's heart of purest gold
E is for God's eyes with love light shining
R means right and right Christ'll always be
Put them all together, they spell MOTHER, a word that means God's love to me.

Paul's Mother

Chorus: "I'm Gonna Sit Right Down And Write Myself A Letter"
She's gonna sit right down and write herself a letter, and make believe it came from Paul. She's gonna write words, oh so nice; she's gonna read them once or twice. A lot of news will be inside. She'll be filled with pride.

She's gonna smile and say, "I hope you're feeling better," and close with love like good sons often do. She's gonna sit right down and write herself a letter and make believe it came from Paul.

Lydia

Chorus: "My Blue Heaven"
When whippoorwill calls and evening is nigh, I hurry to my purple heaven. A turn to the right, a little white light, will lead you to my purple heaven.

Lydia

Chorus: "It's A Long Way To Tipperary"
There's a home in Thyatria, far across the River Mazitza. Near the plains of Philippi, where purple is the dye. There lives Lydia and her servants who are anything but shy. There's a home in Thyatria, where purple is the dye.

Dorcas

Chorus: "Quilting Party"
In the sky the bright stars glitter. On the bank the pale moon
shines. It is in the city of Joppa that we are sewing purple quilts.
We are sewing purple quilts, we are sewing purple quilts. It
is in the home of Dorcas that we are sewing purple quilts.

Chorus: "Row, Row, Row Your Boat"
Sew, Sew, Sew your seams in a nice straight line;
Sewing, sewing, sewing, sewing takes up all my time!

Narrator

8

A Sundae Treat

Leader's Helps

"A Sundae Treat" can take on a double meaning if done on a "Sunday" afternoon or evening. This resource can be used for a youth gathering, family event, congregational night, or women's program. What fun it will be to gather for worship, a special program, reflection time, and then make your own ice cream creation.

If used for an afternoon event, the following may serve as an example for the order of the day:

Menu of the Day

1:45-2:00	May we take your order? Registration
2:00-2:15	Here's your special dish! Opening Worship
2:15-3:15	Peel those bananas! Main speaker or special group
3:15-3:45	Scoop that ice cream and add those toppings! Build your own banana split or ice cream sundae. Add a sprinkling of old and new friendships and lots of Christian fellowship!
3:45-4:00	A great topping! Closing Worship

Have available toppings and fruit to build ice cream sundaes and banana splits. Name tags such as the ones included on the next page may be used.

Bulletin

A Sundae Treat
(Name of Event)

The Main Bananas
(Group in charge/Guest speaker/Program title)

A Variety Of Flavors
(Name of participants in the program/Groups represented/Agenda for the event)

Yummy Toppings
Fun!
Fellowship!
Worship!
Program!
Friendships!
Building Christian Community!
Joy in the Lord!

Menu Of The Day
Registration and name tags: May we take your order?

Opening Worship: Here's your special dish!

Main program: Peel those bananas!
(Guest speaker, group, music, promotional, puppet show, readings, and so forth)

Fellowship: Scoop that ice cream and add those toppings! Build your own banana split or ice cream sundae. Add a sprinkling of old and new friendships and lots of Christian fellowship!

Closing Worship: A great topping!

Program Format

A Sundae Treat

Opening Worship
Greeting and introductions
Hymn
Opening Prayer
Your Special Biblical Dish (*see pages 85-88*)
Song/Special Music

Optional Program Suggestions (*see page 88*)

Closing Worship
Announcements
Offering and Offertory
Prayers
The Lord's Prayer
Closing Remarks and Benediction (*see page 88*)
Hymn

Program

Your Special Biblical Dish — A Biblical Reflection

Preparation: This is the opportunity to insert biblical passages as you build a banana split. Have pieces cut out before hand (*see page 89*). A reader or readers may read the scripture passages. Try to involve as many participants as possible. The leader places the objects on an easel, board or flannelgraph and reflects on each item.

Leader: Today we have gathered to worship our Lord, to hear from God's Word, to reflect upon its meaning in our lives, and to enjoy a special fellowship by creating some delicious ice cream concoctions. We begin by hearing from our first reader.

Reader 1: Hebrews 11:1-3

Leader: We begin to create our Sundae Treat by placing as our bowl — FAITH (*Bowl labeled FAITH put up*). The writer of Hebrews tells us that we gain understanding only through faith. God spoke in the beginning, and the world was formed. The invisible became visible. It is by faith we receive Jesus Christ as Lord. What was hidden and invisible to our understanding before that time, now becomes revealed through the power of the Holy Spirit. With faith we then begin to hope and know that we have the assurance that God is in control of our lives. Conviction comes as we exercise that faith, trusting in God to deliver according to his perfect will. Faith — the bowl into which we now put the rest of our sundae. We walk in faith through this life, led by God's Holy Spirit as we give up the desires of the flesh. Hear how this is accomplished.

Reader 2: Galatians 5:13-25

Leader: We add our bananas — the FRUIT OF THE SPIRIT (*Put a banana labeled FRUIT OF THE SPIRIT on top of the bowl*). This fruit is manifested in our lives as we die to self and allow Christ to live in our hearts. Love, joy, peace, patience, kindness, goodness, faithfulness, humility, and self-control (*Add bunches of bananas marked with these fruits next to bowl*): They all don't arrive at once. Each comes as we allow the Holy Spirit to work in all areas of our lives. As we pray, and ask God for this fruit, each will come forth at the right time. No one enjoys green bananas, and no one enjoys overripe fruit either. God's fruit is always just right and badly needed in all of our lives. As bananas are loaded with potassium, so the fruit of the Holy Spirit is loaded with what we need to live a life of faith. But what does Jesus say we need next?

Reader 3: John 14:16-21

Leader: The role of the Holy Spirit in our lives is to reveal the truth to us. This truth is that God so loved us — each one individually and specially — that he sent Jesus to save us from our sins. The Spirit opens our minds to this truth and to receive God's love. And so we build our ice cream sundae — with a scoop of the Father, who created us in his image and loves us, a scoop of Jesus, who came as our Lord and our Savior, and a scoop of the Holy Spirit, our helper through life and the one who shows us the Father's love through Christ (*Add a chocolate scoop of ice cream marked FATHER, a vanilla scoop marked SON, and a strawberry scoop marked HOLY SPIRIT*). Next we add the toppings to these basics before us.

Reader 4: Jude 20; 2 Timothy 3:16

Leader: Our banana split would not be complete without some whipped topping (*Add whipped topping marked with Christian*

Community, Prayer, Scripture, and Service). And so we add Jude 20 which calls us to build ourselves up in Christian community through faith and prayer and 2 Timothy which tells us how to do this. As we study the scripture we teach, rebuke, correct and train ourselves and others so that all may be equipped for service. But our concoction needs some extras, and so we add our next toppings.

Reader 5: John 4:24; 1 John 1:7

Leader: Crushed oreo cookies, M & M's, Reese's pieces, and the like are added ingredients which make our sundaes special. John tells us to allow the Holy Spirit to help us worship. As we ask God's Spirit to move in our hearts, our hearts respond in true worship to Christ for all he has done for us. Walking in that truth, we have the light of Christ shining from us to others. Then we participate in fellowship with God and one another. What fun it is then to enjoy that abundant life in Christ! And so we add our unique toppings of worship, fellowship and fun in Christ (*Add sprinkles marked accordingly*). So what is next in our ice cream biblical creation?

Reader 6: 1 Corinthians 15:1-11

Leader: Saint Paul's confession is ours also — the GOOD NEWS of salvation (*Top with whipped topping, sprinkles and chocolate sauce marked GOOD NEWS*). Our hot fudge topping we label GOOD NEWS. This message of salvation has been passed on to us through generations of faithful witnesses through the power of the Holy Spirit. When we hear of God's grace poured out to us in the birth, death, and resurrection of Christ, we respond through the Holy Spirit in belief. Then we have new life — a life centered in God's love manifested in his Son, Jesus our Savior and Lord. Let us hear of that love from our final reader.

Reader 7: 1 John 4:7-16

Leader: Our final reading tops off our banana split sundae treat — LOVE, God's cherry (*Top chocolate GOOD NEWS with cherry labeled LOVE*). God is love. Jesus is God's love for us. The Holy Spirit, given to us in our baptism and manifested daily in our response to God's grace, enables us to love our Lord and others in his name. As we receive God's love, we see Christ in our neighbor and become Christ to others. Continue to be filled with the love of the Lord and share it with others. Indulge daily in this creation that God has placed before us now and go forth to share all you have partaken of with others. Amen.

Suggested Closing Remarks And Benediction

Leader: We hope that you will cherish this time as one where you were treated to the flavor of Christ in your life as you have experienced him in worship, our program, and fellowship with others. May you continue to be fed by God's presence and the love God gives you for each other. Go in peace and enjoy Jesus. He is a treat not just meant for Sunday — S - U - N - D - A - Y — but for every day of your entire life. Go in peace and serve the Lord.

Response: Thanks be to God!

Optional Program Ideas

Invite a special speaker or group to come in for this day. If puppeteers or clowns are available use them. Other shorter options might be the use of the following children's materials.

Option 1: Read the children's book, *Where The Wild Things Are,* by Maurice Sendak. Follow this up by a reading from Romans 8:28-39 and reflect on this children's story of how we often do the things we don't want to do, but that nothing separates us from the love of God.

Option 2: Read *Love You Forever* by Robert Munsch. Extras may act out this delightful story of a mother's love for a son from birth to maturity to the birth of his own child.

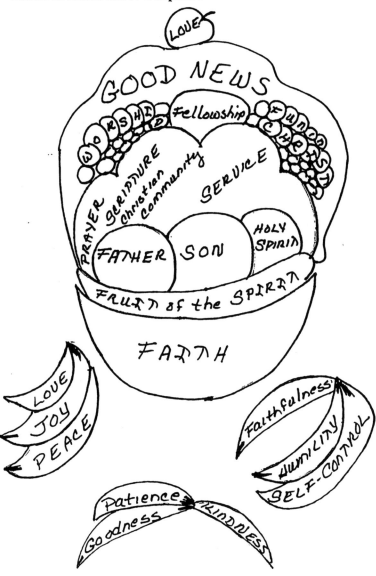

LOVE

GOOD NEWS

WORSHIP   Fellowship   HONOR CHRIST

PRAYER   SCRIPTURE   Christian community   SERVICE

FATHER   SON   HOLY SPIRIT

FRUIT of the SPIRIT

FAITH

LOVE   JOY   PEACE

Faithfulness   HUMILITY   SELF-CONTROL

Patience   KINDNESS   Goodness

9

God's Picnic Basket

Leader's Helps

"God's Picnic Basket" is a good program for June, July, or August. It may be used as a congregational or women's program. Reader 1 may read the congregation's mission statement or the women's purpose statement. The program requires a leader and 13 readers. Readers may be drawn from the audience. Readings should be printed out for the individuals as suggested below.

Reader 1: Read Mission or Organization's Purpose Statement

Reader 2: Hebrews 10:24-25
"Let us consider how to provoke one another to love and good deeds, not neglecting to meet together, as is the habit of some, but encouraging one another, and all the more as you see the Day approaching."

Reader 3: 2 Timothy 3:16-17
"All scripture is inspired by God and is useful for teaching, for reproof, for correction, and for training in righteousness, so that everyone who belongs to God may be proficient, thoroughly equipped for every good work."

Reader 4: 2 Corinthians 13:11-14
"Finally, brothers and sisters, farewell. Put things in order, listen to my appeal, agree with one another, live in peace; and the God of love and peace will be with you. Greet one another with a holy kiss. All the saints greet you. The grace of the Lord Jesus Christ, the love of God and the communion of the Holy Spirit be with all of you."

Reader 5: Luke 22:19

"Then he took a loaf of bread, and when he had given thanks he broke it, and gave it to them, saying, 'This is my body, which is given for you. Do this in remembrance of me.' "

Reader 6: Ephesians 6:10, 18

"Be strong in the Lord and in the strength of his mighty power. Pray in the Spirit at all times in every prayer and supplication. To that end keep alert and always persevere in supplication for all the saints."

Reader 7: 1 Corinthians 12:7-11

"To each is given the manifestation of the Spirit for the common good. To one is given through the Spirit the utterance of wisdom, and to another the utterance of knowledge according to the same Spirit, to another faith by the same Spirit, to another gifts of healing by the one Spirit, to another the working of miracles, to another prophecy, to another the discernment of spirits, to another various kinds of tongues, to another the interpretation of tongues. All these are activated by one and the same Spirit, who allots to each one individually just as the Spirit chooses."

Reader 8: Galatians 5:22-23

"By contrast, the fruit of the Spirit is love, joy, peace, patience, kindness, generosity, faithfulness, gentleness and self-control. There is no law against such things."

Reader 9: Hebrews 5:11-14

"About this we have much to say that is hard to explain, since you have become dull in understanding. For though by this time you ought to be teachers, you need someone to teach you again the basic elements of the oracles of God. You need milk, not solid food; for everyone who lives on milk, being still an infant, is unskilled in the word of righteousness. But solid food is for the mature, for those whose faculties have been trained by practice to distinguish good from evil."

Reader 10: 1 John 4:11-12

"Beloved, since God loved us so much, we also ought to love one another. No one has ever seen God; if we love one another, God lives in us, and his love is perfected in us."

Reader 11: Revelation 21:3-4

"And I heard a loud voice from the throne saying, 'See, the home of God is among mortals. He will dwell with them as their God; they will be his peoples, and God himself will be with them; he will wipe every tear from their eyes. Death will be no more; mourning and crying and pain will be no more, for the first things have passed away.' "

Reader 12: Ephesians 6:11-17

"Put on the whole armor of God, so that you may be able to stand against the wiles of the devil. For our struggle is not against enemies of blood and flesh, but against the rulers, against the authorities, against the cosmic powers of this present darkness, against the spiritual forces of evil in the heavenly places. Therefore take up the whole armor of God, so that you may be able to withstand on that evil day, and having done everything, to stand firm. Stand therefore, and fasten the belt of truth around your waist, and put on the breastplate of righteousness. As shoes for your feet put on whatever will make you ready to proclaim the gospel of peace. With all of these, take the shield of faith, with which you will be able to quench all the flaming arrows of the evil one. Take the helmet of salvation, and the sword of the Spirit, which is the Word of God."

Reader 13: 2 Timothy 4:2-4

"I solemnly urge you: proclaim the message; be persistent whether the time is favorable or unfavorable; convince, rebuke, and encourage, with the utmost patience in teaching. For the time is coming when people will not put up with sound doctrine, but having itching ears, they will accumulate for themselves teachers to suit their own desires, and will turn away from listening to the truth and wander away to myths."

Props Needed By Leader
Picnic basket with name of congregation/organization on it
Checkered tablecloth
Paper plate, holder, and silverware
Ceramic coffee mug
Hot dog bun
Hot dog
Catsup, mustard, and relish
Bowl of fruit
Kentucky Fried Chicken bucket or picture of chicken and dish
    of potato salad
Serving spoon
Dessert
Napkin
Umbrella
Suntan lotion
Can of Off
Cut-out picture of an ant
Bottle of Joy dishwashing liquid
Chalice and communion wafer
Jug of lemonade

Program

Leader: Summer's here. Time to get outdoors. Time to bask in the warmth of the sun and enjoy fellowship with God and one another. As good congregational members (or members of this women's organization), that fellowship usually involves food and a little instruction in the faith. So today, we are going to go on a picnic with God and each other.

Now we need to look at what will make this picnic a successful event. First of all, we should have something to carry our picnic items in. For us it is our congregation (or organization) which is represented by this picnic basket. (*Turn basket around so sign with church/organization name on it shows*) This is not just another social group or community club we belong to. It is one with purpose and meaning. Hear our mission statement (or purpose statement of organization).

Reader 1: Read Mission/Purpose Statement

Leader: With our purpose in mind, let's take a look inside our basket and see what God has for us to make this a special time of learning and fellowship.

(*Pull out checkered tablecloth*) First we'll spread out a tablecloth so that we have a clean area to eat from. For us that is the Church. Hear what the Word of God has to say concerning Christ's Church from the Book of Hebrews 10:24-25.

Reader 2: "Let us consider how to provoke one another to love and good deeds, not neglecting to meet together, as is the habit of some, but encouraging one another, and all the more as you see the Day approaching."

Leader: As we gather within the Church for times of worship, monthly meetings, special events and programs such as Mother's

Day Salad Suppers, Christmas Teas, and the like, we encourage each other, for we have come under the headship of our Lord and Savior, seeking his will in the life of the Church and our congregational units. We spur one another on by our faithfulness in attending these events.

Let's see what else God has in his picnic basket. (*Pull out paper plate and holder and silverware*) Of course, we need something to eat off of and with. For us that is good, solid teaching from the Word of God. Hear what Timothy has to say about this in 2 Timothy 3:16-17.

Reader 3: "All scripture is inspired by God and is useful for teaching, for reproof, for correction, and for training in righteousness, so that everyone who belongs to God may be proficient, equipped for every good work."

Leader: We have many in our congregation (organization) who help make this a reality for us. Our greater church-wide organization employs many staff people who channel good programs and studies to us. But let's see what else God has in his basket. (*Pull out a coffee mug*) What would our congregation (organization) be without its coffee? Of course, served in a ceramic mug and not plastic foam! This cup represents the fellowship we enjoy with each other. Our circle meetings, our study groups, our activities such as quilting, putting layettes, health care, and school kits together, mission projects, and so much more. We come together in Christ to share with one another a special Christian fellowship. Hear what Saint Paul tells us about fellowship from 2 Corinthians 13:11-14.

Reader 4: "Finally, brothers and sisters, farewell. Put things in order, listen to my appeal, agree with one another, live in peace; and the God of love and peace will be with you. Greet one another with a holy kiss. All the saints greet you. The grace of the Lord Jesus Christ, the love of God, and the communion of the Holy Spirit be with all of you."

Leader: One of the signs of a group that promotes healthy fellowship is all that hugging it shows to each of its participants. Fellowship in the Spirit is a must for our picnic lunch.

What do we have next? (*Pull out a hot dog bun*) Bread. When we come together in fellowship, we remember the many times our Lord Jesus took bread, gave thanks and offered it to his disciples. Hear a passage from Luke 22:19.

Reader 5: "Then he took a loaf of bread, and when he had given thanks he broke it, and gave it to them, saying, 'This is my body, which is given for you. Do this in remembrance of me.' "

Leader: When we break bread together, we share in communion with God through Jesus Christ our Lord. We remember his sacrifice for our sins. Our Lord did a lot of eating with his followers, and so should we. For it is in the breaking of bread with one another that we nurture and encourage each other in daily life. Jesus is the living bread we feast on each day which nourishes our spirits and enables us to grow in faith.

And what should go into this bun? (*Pull out a hot dog*) Now teaching is important. Fellowship is great. Taking communion each opportunity we have brings us closer to God. But another key ingredient to our picnic is prayer. Hear what Saint Paul tells us in Ephesians 6:10 and 18.

Reader 6: "Be strong in the Lord and in the strength of his mighty power. Pray in the Spirit at all times in every prayer and supplication. To that end keep alert and always persevere in supplication for all the saints."

Leader: God wants us on a steady diet of prayer. As we grow stronger in the Lord and his mighty power through the discipline of prayer, God will stir spiritual gifts up within us. But no hot dog is complete without its condiments — catsup, mustard, and relish. (*Pull condiments out*) For the Christian these relishes are served up in our midst as spiritual gifts. These gifts are manifested in a variety of ways. Saint Paul lists some of these in 1 Corinthians 12:7-11.

Reader 7: "To each is given the manifestation of the Spirit for the common good. To one is given through the Spirit the utterance of wisdom, and to another the utterance of knowledge according to that same Spirit, to another faith by the same Spirit, to another gifts of healing by the one Spirit, to another the working of miracles, to another prophecy, to another the discernment of spirits, to another various kinds of tongues, to another the interpretation of tongues. All these are activated by one and the same Spirit, who allots to each one individually just as the Spirit chooses."

Leader: Now many may like their hot dogs with just mustard. Some choose to add onion and really spice up that prayer life. God knows what his body, the Church, needs. He will manifest the gifts of the Spirit in order to build it up, but he calls to us to desire spiritual gifts so that the body may be healed and grow.

Along with the gifts, God wants us to picnic on the fruits. So, the Spirit has provided us with a fruit salad from the original recipe book, the Bible, titled Galatians 5:22-23. (*Bring out bowl of fruit*)

Reader 8: "By contrast, the fruit of the Spirit is love, joy, peace, patience, kindness, generosity, faithfulness, gentleness and self-control. There is no law against such things."

Leader: As the Spirit of God indwells the believer, the acts of the sinful nature — sexual immorality, impurity, licentiousness, idolatry, sorcery, enmities, strife, jealousy, anger, dissension, factions, envy, drunkenness, carousing and things like these — will be replaced by the fruit of the Jesus living within.

But just one hot dog with a bun and a cup of coffee will not really fill us up. Will it? We need more substance. How about some fried chicken and potato salad? (*Pull out a bucket from KFC or a picture of a chicken and a dish of potato salad*) Saint Peter reminds us that we need to grow up in the faith. From his letter to the Hebrews 5:11-14 we read.

Reader 9: "About this we have much to say that is hard to explain, since you have become dull in understanding. For though by this time you ought to be teachers, you need someone to teach you again the basic elements of the oracles of God. You need milk, not solid food; for everyone who lives on milk, being still an infant, is unskilled in the word of righteousness. But solid food is for the mature, for those whose faculties have been trained by practice to distinguish good from evil."

Leader: We need to saturate ourselves in the Word. Through personal Bible reading, participating in our congregational and organizational Bible studies, and the like, we will grow in our knowledge of God by being exposed to the Holy Scriptures and chewing on the meat of that Word. But many choose to only nibble on a leg or wing. Others want to sink their teeth more fully into a thigh or breast. It is up to the individual how much she wishes to consume. The Word enables us to understand what Christ desires from us, his children. But we need a spoon to serve up our potato salad. (*Pull out spoon*) Hear what John tells us to serve our faith up with. A reading from 1 John 4:11-12.

Reader 10: "Beloved, since God loved us so much, we also ought to love one another. No one has ever seen God; if we love one another, God lives in us, and his love is perfected in us."

Leader: So we dish up and serve God's love to others along with teaching, fellowship, breaking of bread, prayer, the spiritual gifts, the fruits of the Spirit, and the study of the Word. Love is also seen in our service, our dessert, of a life lived in union with Christ. (*Take out a dessert*)

Christ took on the very nature of a servant and ministered to those in his midst. God calls us to respond likewise by serving others and showing the world his love. Ephesians 6:7-8 tells us to "render service with enthusiasm, as to the Lord and not to men and women, knowing that whatever good we do, we will receive the same again from the Lord, whether we are slaves or free."

We come together in our local congregational units to quilt for relief victims, to support our spouse abuse centers and caring houses, to give to those less privileged than ourselves, to reach out in Christ's love to those hurting in our midst. As we enthusiastically respond to the grace we have been blessed with in Jesus, our acts of service become acts of devotion to God for his Son. These are desserts — for others are treated to special blessings because of our response to Christ. Through our actions, our involvement in community, and our personal growth, we are enabled to reach out for Christ in love and service.

(*Pull out napkin*) Having feasted, we take out our napkin and brush the crumbs away. The napkin can also be used to dab our eyes and brush the tears away. For some of the picnics we go on in life are filled with struggle and suffering. Many tears are shed at times, but God is there in the midst of the sunny days as well as the rainy. (*Pull out umbrella*) Hear what John tells us in the Book of Revelation 21:3-4.

Reader 11: "And I heard a loud voice from the throne saying, 'See, the home of God is among mortals. He will dwell with them as their God; they will be his peoples, and God himself will be with them; he will wipe every tear from their eyes. Death will be no more; mourning and crying and pain will be no more, for the first things have passed away.' "

Leader: God does not send us on picnics alone or unprotected. There is a host of heaven who accompanies us, and he has equipped us with a special suntan oil called the Armor of God found in Ephesians 6:11-17 which protects us. (*Pull out suntan lotion*)

Reader 12: "Put on the whole armor of God, so that you may be able to stand against the wiles of the devil. For our struggle is not against enemies of blood and flesh, but against the rulers, against the authorities, against the cosmic powers of this present darkness, against the spiritual forces of evil in the heavenly places. Therefore, take up the whole armor of God, so that you may be able to withstand on that evil day, and having done everything, to stand firm. Stand therefore, and fasten the belt of truth around your waist, and put on the breastplate of righteousness. As shoes for your feet put on whatever will make you ready to proclaim the gospel of peace. With all of these, take the shield of faith, with which you will be able to quench all the flaming arrows of the evil one. Take the helmet of salvation, and the sword of the Spirit, which is the Word of God."

Leader: We need to use our Off (*Pull out can of Off*) to repel the fiery darts of the evil one. For 2 Timothy warns us in chapter 4:2-4 of the mosquitoes which will fly around our heads and buzz in our ears.

Reader 13: "I solemnly urge you: proclaim the message; be persistent whether the time is favorable or unfavorable; convince, rebuke, and encourage, with the utmost patience in teaching. For the time is coming when people will not put up with sound doctrine, but having itching ears, they will accumulate for themselves teachers to suit their own desires, and will turn away from listening to the truth and wander away to myths."

Leader: We need to be so well grounded in the Word and exercising the power of prayer that we will be able to stand firm and not be carried away by the invading hosts of Satan. (*Pull out ant*) The ants will come marching into our lives, one by one, two by two, to make our picnic in life less than glorious, seeking to draw us away from lives lived out in faithfulness to God and committed to the Lord Jesus Christ.

But God is present, continually drawing us back into fellowship with him and one another through his body the Church. (*Pull out bottle of Joy dishwashing liquid*) The joy of the Lord is our strength. As we take our picnic stuff back and do the dishes, we are reminded that through our baptism our sins are washed away, making us squeaky clean through the precious blood of Jesus our Savior. (*Pull out Chalice and wafer*) Communion restores us to that forgiven state as we remember God's love and Jesus' sacrifice. Through union with God, we are empowered by the Spirit to go out into life and picnic — no matter what the weather.

So may your summer and your lives be continual picnics with the One who is our constant companion and friend. For what type of picnic would it be without someone to share it with? And Jesus and your brothers and sisters in Christ are great companions! So, pass the lemonade. (*Pull out jug*) It's "Picnic Time!"

10

The Armor Of God

Leader's Helps

This humorous but educational program can be used within the church at any time of the year. "The Armor Of God — Style Show For This Present Day" is a skit based on Ephesians 6:10-17.

A narrator goes through introducing each model and what each is wearing. Props and articles may be made accordingly. A pianist may play some quiet accompaniment for those modeling.

Model 1: The Belt Of Truth
Model 2: The Breastplate Of Righteousness
Model 3: Gospel Shoes
Model 4: Shield Of Faith
Model 5: The Helmet Of Salvation
Model 6: The Sword Of The Holy Spirit

"Onward Christian Soldiers" may be sung as an opening for this skit. After the skit, a reader may share from Ephesians 6:10-20. Discussion on spiritual warfare may be added using the handout on "The Prayer Warrior." "Stand Up, Stand Up, For Jesus" may be the final hymn for the night.

Select participants from your congregation who are not usually tapped for programs. This resource may be used by Sunday schools, youth groups, women's organizations or special worship service opportunities.

Protection for God's Prayer Warrior
Ephesians 6:10-18

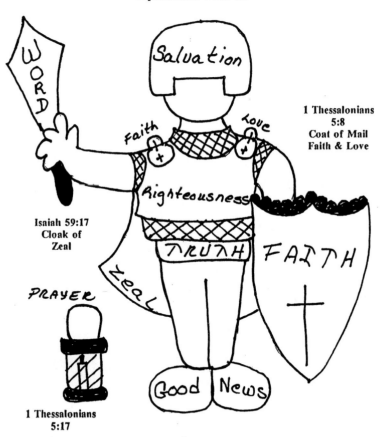

1 Thessalonians
5:8
Coat of Mail
Faith & Love

Isaiah 59:17
Cloak of
Zeal

1 Thessalonians
5:17

Program

A Style Show For This Present Day

Narrator: With the change of seasons comes a change in style. Being "stylish," that is "in vogue," is what the world says we should do. As Christians, we should look good, so the clothing which our Lord provides looks smart and never goes out of style. It is durable, beautiful, exciting, and right up to date! So, today we would like to present to you, direct from the King of kings himself, a style show from the Word of God. The items you will see presented here are available to each of you and are essentials to the basic wardrobe of every Christian.

Model 1. Our first model, (name), comes to us from the lively metropolis of (town) where she has captured many an eye as she has reflected the love of Christ. She takes a firm stand before us now so all can see her beautiful belt. She has buckled it securely around her waist. This item is called the **Belt Of Truth**. Notice how this belt shines. It casts a light out to those around, especially those living in darkness. This truth, which our model proudly wears, is a "liberating" truth. It sets the wearer free from sin. As Jesus came to witness the truth, so everyone who belongs to the truth hears his voice. In this truth, the devil cannot stand, for truth is not in him. Therefore, as you wear this beautiful belt around you each day, know that you will be able to stand firm in the solid and firm reality of a God who loves, has rescued you, and given you salvation by faith. The cost of this first item is forsaking falsehood and sin and responding to the saving knowledge of the truth of Jesus Christ as Lord and Savior.

Model 2. Our next model, (name), is also from the booming metropolis of Christian faith (name of church). She proudly wears a most stylish item — the **Breastplate Of Righteousness.** Notice how firmly in place this garment is. In the Old Testament the breastplate symbolized the function of the high priest as representative of all Israel. That breastplate was made of gold, violet, purple, and scarlet thread woven into linen which was then folded double into a square. In it were set 12 precious stones in four rows of three, each engraved with one of the 12 tribes. The high priest was chosen to stand in the gap for his people. 1 Peter 2:9 says that we are "a chosen people, a royal priesthood." We need this garment to "declare the praises of him who called you out of the darkness into his wonderful light." By sporting this article, we will have that "innocent" look. Our conduct, when wearing this item, will be morally right and proper. This piece is costly, for it is bought by being right with God, being saved and vindicated through Christ. Therefore, we will proudly boast when we wear it — not in achieving it by our works — but in the fact that God alone has caused this free gift to be firmly established in place in our lives by grace.

Model 3. Next we have "Twinkle Toes" (name) from over on (give street or road name). Notice how light on her feet she is. That is because she has been especially fitted by God with the **Readiness** that comes from the **Gospel Of Peace.** She is eager to be about spreading the Good News. These **Gospel Shoes** she wears are not cumbersome or tight. They do not bind or restrict the wearer in any way, but enable her to be about the manufacturer's business with flexibility, knowing that the Lord is guiding her footsteps every step of the way. Wearing these shoes brings such wonderful benefits, not only to the wearer, but also to those she chooses to dance with, for her peace is contagious. Others want to know how they, too, can obtain it. How? By purchasing this item with a full surrender of self to the One who surrendered all for you, Jesus Christ. Thank you, (name).

106

Model 4. Watch out! Here comes (name). (Name) steps forth valiantly and forcefully into our spotlight wielding the **Shield Of Faith.** This is an essential item in your Christian wardrobe, and one which you should not venture forth into the world's arena without. As Christians, we engage in spiritual warfare. This long, oblong shield will help you to extinguish the flaming arrows and fiery darts of the evil one who will surely attack you as you go forth to battle the powers of darkness in Christ's name. This article will never be out of style, for faith looks not only to the past — the work begun by Jesus' redeeming death and glorious resurrection — but to the future — our eternal life with him. Faith is a precious gift of God, so value the faith given to each of you to wield and to overcome the powers of sin. We are nearing the end of our style show presented by God to you and available from the Creator upon request. Only two more beautiful models to go.

Model 5. And here comes (name). (Name) is crowned with the most expensive item on our list. It is beyond cost. Upon her head she wears the **Helmet Of Salvation.** Notice how tightly and securely this article fits her head. It covers so completely that there is no room for doubt or unbelief to creep in once it is securely in place. The color is red — the precious blood shed for each of us by Jesus on Calvary. The crosses across the front symbolize the death of the purchaser. It is his emblem to us. His label which was so costly. By wearing this helmet, we have knowledge of Jesus as Lord and his will for our lives. By all means, purchase this item first.

Model 6. And finally, we have beautiful, dainty (name), brandishing the **Sword Of The Spirit.** Notice how easily she swings this item. She and the item have become one. This is a must also for each of you, for it is the Word of God, sharper than a two-edged sword, penetrating the innermost part of a person. It will confound Christ's enemies. It is an offensive as well as a defensive weapon. It will force every person it makes contact with to a decision by stripping them of pretense and excuse. Wield this article through the power of God's Holy Spirit. Know it well! Make it a part of your very being. It has electrifying power. The cost — time in study, prayer, and reflection.

Narrator: (*Models now come out together*) Now all of these items — the Belt Of Truth, the Breastplate Of Righteousness, Feet Shod In The Gospel Of Peace, the Shield Of Faith, the Helmet Of Salvation, and the Sword Of The Holy Spirit — come together to make one complete and essential outfit for every Christian believer's basic wardrobe. We have titled this creation "The Full Armor of God." Don't be without any of these articles seen here today. Make sure you have them for your own wardrobe. Purchase each and wear the ensemble boldly as a witness to your faith in Christ Jesus as Lord. Attire yourself every day of your life with each article so that you will always be properly clothed and fully equipped as a beautiful, overcoming child of the King!

11

Just Look At All Those Trees!

Leader's Helps

As a fall program, "Just Look At All Those Trees!" journeys through an exploration of trees in scripture beginning in the Garden of Eden and ending in that garden to show how God expelled humankind for their own protection but through his grace brought them back once more to taste of the gift of eternal life found in the Cross of Christ.

This program involves a leader who introduces the program and then concludes it. Six readers are required.

Reader 1: Introduces the Garden of Eden and the Tree of Life and the Tree of the Knowledge of Good and Evil. A bitten apple, a flaming sword, and a sign "Closed for Own Good" are placed on board by reader also.

Reader 2: Introduces the cypress tree as God's CARING TREE. Places cypress tree on board and covers it after with sign, CARING.

Reader 3: Introduces the oak tree as God's TREE OF ORDER. Places oak tree next to cypress and covers it after with sign, ORDER.

Reader 4: Introduces the poplar tree as God's TREE OF PROMISE. Places poplar tree next to cypress and covers it after with sign, PROMISE.

Reader 5: Introduces the weeping willow tree as God's TREE OF WISDOM. Places willow next to poplar and covers it after with sign, WISDOM.

Reader 6: Introduces the palm tree as God's TREE OF PASSION. Places palm next to willow and covers it after with sign, PASSION.

Leader: Introduces the program and concludes it by placing the Cross as a tree next to the palm. Puts sign, CURSE, over the Cross. Directs attention back to the Garden of Eden. Sign, "Now Open," placed over sign, "Closed for Own Good." Put sign, ETERNAL LIFE, over Tree of Life.

Suggested hymn for introduction: "There Is A Balm In Gilead"

Suggested hymn for conclusion: "Thine Is The Glory" or "In The Cross Of Christ I Glory"

This program is an excellent resource for a fall kick-off for a congregation's women's, youth, or intergenerational night. Participants may be invited to a potluck meal followed by this program. Goal of the program: to create a warm night of fellowship and learn of God's grace and love for those involved.

Program

Leader: Fall — a wonderful time to be out in nature. The coolness of the breeze, dispelling the heat of summer, brings a surge of refreshment to the soul. God is so evident in his creation at this time as the autumn leaves display their beauty. Fall color tours, football games, camping excursions, long hikes in parks and woods, all draw us closer to the Lord of Creation as we witness his hand in the beauty of the outdoors. The red, orange, brown, and gold of the turning leaves bring enjoyment to the eyes. The crunching beneath our feet as we walk and the rustling of fallen leaves blowing around our yards sound sweet to the ears. The toughening of hands, diligently raking that yard filled with nature's debris, makes one well aware of touch. As the piles grow, the odor of decomposition increases. The nose might also pick up that wonderful smell of burning leaves, brush, and wood which often signals the end of summer. All senses seem to be heightened at this time — even taste as cider and crisp apples are enjoyed. Our sight, hearing, touch, smell, and taste come together to focus our attention on the season. We stand in awe of God at work as we look at all those trees!

God has been at work in nature since time began. The wonders he has created for his creatures to enjoy are breathtaking. Fall brings them alive for us. But behind those creations — especially his trees — God has a message for us today. And so we take this time to look at the trees in selected passages in the Word.

Reader 1 (Garden of Eden, Tree of Life, Tree of the Knowledge of Good and Evil): To begin with, we go straight to Genesis. The Lord God started big and splashy: his showcase — the Garden of Eden. (*Put up sign* — GARDEN OF EDEN) Here God placed Adam and Eve and provided for their every need. In Genesis 2:8 we see that God made to grow every tree that

111

is pleasant to the sight and good for food. What a great provider! The eye saw a variety of foliage and beauty, and the taste buds were treated to an excellent assortment of fruit. Along with these trees, God planted in the midst of the garden two special trees: the tree of life and the tree of the knowledge of good and evil. (*Plant these two trees in garden*) Now the first trees were given to man and woman to eat from, but God strictly forbid them to eat from the tree of knowledge of good and evil. All the other trees the couple could look at and enjoy, but this tree was off limits!

We all know the rest of this story, as Paul Harvey would say. The forbidden tree was just too appealing. Once having eaten its fruit (*Put bitten apple on tree*), the couple became aware not only of good, which had always surrounded them, but of evil. Disobedience entered the world, and sin began to destroy humankind.

But God loved his creations so that he did not destroy them. Now knowing good and evil, God feared that his creations would reach out and take the fruit from the tree of life, eat, and live forever. For their own protection they were driven from the garden. A guard was set before the Garden of Eden with a flaming sword (*Put flaming sword on board and sign "Closed For Own Good" over Garden of Eden*) to turn away those who sought to eat of the tree of life. And so we plant in our garden forest a guard before these first biblical trees. Before the closed door to this garden we turn away, like our first parents, saddened and feeling abandoned.

Reader 2 (Cypress Tree): However, God did not abandon his first children nor has he abandoned us. Yet death, which is so evident in the falling of our autumn leaves, came into the world to protect us. And God continues to use trees to focus attention on his protection. Look at the tree in Genesis 6. (*Put cypress tree on board*) The world had gotten so bad, God set out to destroy it. But salvation came in the form of a tree. Noah built an ark out of cypress wood and covered it with pitch. Now this tree is an evergreen which is valuable in carpentry and building. Some of its hard, red wood is used in making shingles. Pitch, the residue distilled from wood, is used in varnish and caulking. The ark, built by human hands using God's material, was a piece of salvation for Noah and his family. The cypress symbolizes God CARING for his people. And so we plant in our fall garden, God's CARING TREE. (*Place CARING sign over tree*)

Reader 3 (Oak Tree): Noah and his family were faithful, but their descendants continued to taste the forbidden fruit of sin. However, God still cares and does not abandon his unfaithful children. The prophet Isaiah points us to another tree — the oak. (*Put oak tree on board*). The leaves of this tree are often made into garlands and used in floral arrangements decorating our homes at this time of year. The little acorn fruit provides nourishment for the busy squirrels storing up for winter. It also symbolizes the promise of bigger things for from a little acorn a mighty oak tree will come if watered and nourished properly. The timber from this hardwood tree is tough and durable. Its beautiful grain makes its use in woodwork and furniture valuable. We hear of the oak in the book of Isaiah, chapter 6, where the prophet speaks of a city which will lie in ruin.

Israel has turned its wandering eyes upon other gods. It has turned from the God of its creation who has nurtured and cared for it. God will not tolerate this from his people. He warns that he will destroy their dwelling place if they continue to travel this road. Their homes will no longer be decorated with garlands of fall leaves or centerpieces because their inhabitants will go into exile. Isaiah asks how long his people would continue to not listen to their God and turn their backs on him. And God responds, "Until cities lie waste without inhabitant, and houses without people, and the land is utterly desolate; until the Lord sends everyone far away, and vast is the emptiness in the midst of the land. Even if a tenth part remain in it, it will be burned again, like a terebinth (a sumac tree) or an oak, whose stump remains standing when it is felled. The holy seed is its stump" (Isaiah 6:11-13).

Salvation is promised to Israel. An acorn of hope, from which the mighty oak of deliverance will come, is planted into the spirit of God's people. We read in Isaiah 11:1: "A shoot shall come out from the stump of Jesse, and a branch shall grow out of his roots." Salvation will come eventually to Israel, the mighty oak of the lineage of King David, the son of Jesse. Order from chaos will be restored in God's time in spite of the unfaithfulness of his people. The holy city and its chosen inhabitants will be chopped down in order for new life to appear. And so, we plant the oak, symbolizing ORDER, in our garden. (*Place ORDER sign over tree*) God's tree of order is important in our lives for it signifies our days are in God's hands and promises will be kept in his time. The fruit of our waiting will be rewarded like the acorn and the stump. We are often impatient in waiting for God's time and order and chafe at circumstances which go against our grain. But look at the grain of the oak which is so beautiful in the finished product. As the master craftsman rubs the wood with the plane, so our Master creates a wonderful piece of workmanship out of the struggles in our lives.

Reader 4 (Poplar Tree): The next tree we'll look at in God's fall lineup is the poplar. (*Put poplar tree on board*) This slender, quick-growing variety of willow includes aspens, cottonwood, tulip tree, white and black poplars, tacamahas (a North American shade tree), and the balsam poplar, also known as balm of Gilead. The gospel hymn, "There Is A Balm In Gilead," talks of the soothing, medicinal qualities of this balsam tree which brings healing to the soul, but is also used in expectorants and cough syrups.

Jeremiah cries out in Jeremiah 8:22, "Is there no balm in Gilead? Is there no physician there?" Like Isaiah, the prophet Jeremiah has seen the spiritual sickness of disobedience, begun in the garden, rob the health of his people Israel. He knows that only by using the tree that God has provided, here in the poplar, will their sick souls be saved. But he is prophetically speaking for we as Christians know that salvation comes

114

through the tree — a tree to be raised at Calvary. The poplar symbolizes God's PROMISE of redemption for his people. (*Place PROMISE sign over tree*)

Reader 5 (Weeping Willow): How God must cry over the many who will not claim the promise of salvation! Our weeping willow expresses God's lament, his anguish, his passion for his unfaithful, unbelieving children. *(Put willow tree on board)* The willow tree has tough, pliable shoots often used in basketry. Moses once floated in a basket down the Nile toward the waiting arms of his salvation, the pharaoh's daughter. The slender, hanging branches of the willow remind us of this barren woman who must have cried many tears because she had no child. But God planted Moses in pharaoh's court in answer to his people's tears. God planted Jesus in Jerusalem as fulfillment of his promise. The God who cared, who waited until all things were in order, who promised to redeem, who heard his people's cries for deliverance, stood before the Holy City and wept. Matthew 23:37-39 records his sorrow: "Jerusalem, Jerusalem, the city that kills the prophets and stones those who are sent to it! How often have I desired to gather your children together as a hen gathers her brood under her wings, and you were not willing! See, your house is left to you desolate. For I tell you, you will not see me again until you say, 'Blessed is the one who comes in the name of the Lord.' "
The wisdom of the ages now stood before the gates of Jerusalem preparing to do the Father's will and wept. And so we plant the weeping willow, God's tree of WISDOM, in our garden. For it is the wisdom of God which confounds the world in the shape of a tree. (*Place WISDOM sign over tree*)

Reader 6 (Palm Tree): The miracles the Messiah had performed, the baskets of loaves and fishes, the raising of the dead, the blind seeing, the many sensory things that the Jews could see yet not understand and which confounded their minds, would be what the crowds would hail as Jesus entered the Holy City. The "Weeping" Lord they could not understand.

The tender shoot, growing out of the stump of Jesse, growing up before them like a root out of dry ground (Isaiah 53:2), they would not recognize. Isaiah's suffering servant they did not want. They wanted an exalted, conquering victor, and so they heralded Christ's entry with branches from the palm. (*Put palm branches on board*)

Now this tropical tree is marked commonly by a simple stem crowned by a fan of large leaves. Certain species of palm trees are of great economic importance, such as the betel coconut, date, oil, rattan, and wax palm. The leaf of the palm has symbolized victory or rejoicing. We read in John 12:12-13 that as Jesus entered the Holy City, the crowds took branches of palm trees and went out to meet him crying, "Hosanna! Blessed is the one who comes in the name of the Lord — the King of Israel."

The Lord entered what we in the church call Holy Week or the Week of our Lord's Passion. For Christ would endure pain, torture, and sufferings as the one who came in the name of the Lord. Salvation came heralded by the palm, and we plant the palm as the tree of PASSION in our garden. (*Place PASSION sign over tree*)

Leader (Cross): And so we see our final tree, the Cross, appear — a tree by which the crucifixion of our Lord and Savior was carried out. The Old Testament tells us in Deuteronomy 21:22 that when one was convicted of a crime punishable by death, he would be hung on a tree. The corpse could not remain there all night but had to be buried that same day. Anyone hung on a tree is under God's curse. And so we plant the tree of Christ in our garden, God's CURSE, which secured our salvation. (*Put CURSE on Cross*) It is this tree which stands before us now making passage to the tree of eternal life possible. (*Put "Now Open" sign over "Closed For Own Good" sign*)

Saint John saw this tree and recorded his vision for us in the final chapter of Revelation. "Then the angel showed me the river of the water of life, bright as crystal, flowing from the throne of God and of the Lamb through the middle of the street of the city. On either side of the river, is the tree of life with its twelve kinds of fruit, producing its fruit each month; and the leaves of the tree are for the healing of the nations. Nothing accursed will be found there any more. But the throne of God and of the Lamb will be in it" (Revelation 22:1-3).

And so in conclusion, we see that the loving God, who created and CARED for us, brought all things into proper ORDER to carry out his PROMISE with WISDOM through his PASSION by making Christ a CURSE for us, has bestowed on us ETERNAL LIFE. (*Point to each tree and place ETER-NAL LIFE sign over Tree of Life*)

Salvation came into the world with Jesus who sacrificed himself upon the Cross — the tree of death which brought life to each of us. We all have tasted from the tree of the knowledge of good and evil. We know we are sinners in need of the grace of God. When we come to the Cross of Christ, we come to the tree which brought death to our Lord but life to his followers.

When you go out for your next autumn walk, remember the trees you planted today and rejoice in the God of your salvation. For he calls to us each day of our life to celebrate life and marvel as we "just look at all those trees!"

12

In Pursuit Of The Right Spirit

Leader's Helps

As Halloween approaches, Christians begin to engage in its celebration. "In Pursuit Of The Right Spirit" is a means of exploring the roots and items which surround this fall event. This program may be used for an alternative to Trick or Treat night in the congregation or presented as a women's or youth program.

Participants include: Sane Sara, the Saintly Saint, and Leapin' Lin, the Lover of Truth. These two do a back and forth delivery involving the audience.

Pumpkin carols may be sung (adapting old tunes to words of songs recognizing this event). Pumpkin carving, bobbing for apples, making cornstalk wreaths, baking cut-out cookies, and the like can be added to make this a night of fun. Decorations and name tags may follow the theme.

Props needed
1. History book
2. New Year's Eve horn blower
3. Ghost cut-out
4. Reaper/scythe
5. Loaf of bread
6. Bundle of wheat
7. Bible
8. Sign — stone tablet with Commandment #1 written on it
9. Red apple
10. Black horse
11. Black cat
12. Jack-o-lantern

13. Carved potato or potato with face marked on it
14. Fire poster
15. 95 Theses scroll
16. Sign — "All Hallow's Eve" written on one side and "Halloween" written on the other
17. Witch hat with WICCA written across it
18. Folded sign with "hidden" written on front and "occult" written on the inside
19. #13 sign
20. Mask
21. LAW card or scroll
22. Broomstick
23. Tube or jar of ointment
24. Big stirring spoon
25. Cauldron or big kettle
26. Bottle of aspirin
27. Doll — representing "Little People"
28. Green clothing or hat
29. Lightning bolt
30. Horseshoe
31. Bell
32. Skeleton cut-out
33. Bat
34. Toad
35. Salt shaker or box
36. Orange sheet of construction paper with LIFE written on back
37. Black sheet of construction paper with DEATH written in white on back
38. Green apple and nuts
39. Baby doll
40. Green cabbage
41. Garfield cat with candy or a Trick or Treat bag
42. Devil mask, trident or figure of devil
43. Cross
44. Feather duster
45. Holy Spirit dove

All these objects can be placed in a large pumpkin garbage bag. The more fragile and heavier ones may be placed in a decorated box up front. Sara and Lin pull these items out as needed. Sara may dress in black and Lin may dress as a brownie/elf.

Program

Sane Sara, the Saintly Spirit: Good evening and welcome to our Halloween program "In Pursuit Of The Right Spirit." I am Sane Sara, the Saintly Spirit, and I am here as your spiritual guide for this program. Our adventure tonight will be guided by God's Holy Spirit as together we pursue the origins surrounding this time of the year. I have a companion who will assist us on this journey. Please welcome with a round of applause our own Leapin' Lin, the Lover of Truth. (*Audience claps as Leapin' Lin arrives with a pumpkin sack of clues*)

Sara: Well, Lin, that's an interesting sack you have strung on your back. You remind me of a certain peddler just opening his pack.

Lin: Different season, Sara, but I do have some interesting goodies inside. Take for instance this history book. (*Opens history book*) Did you know for instance that the Irish, Welsh, Scots, and English are descendants of the ancient Celts, called the Gauls and Britons? Did you know that their pagan priests were called Druids?

Sara: You mean these people were worshipping other gods before Jesus?

Lin: Correct, especially on October 31, which was considered the Celtic New Year. (*Takes horn blower out*)

Sara: I remember my Latin teacher talking about Julius Caesar recording the "unspeakable" sacrifices the Druids offered up on that night. What does your book say the Celts believed happened on this night?

122

Lin: That the spirits of wicked souls were released.

Sara: (*Pulls ghost from bag*) You mean like in the forms of ghosts, goblins, evil pookas, witches, fairies, elves, ghouls, demons, and the like?

Lin: Yes, and their fearsome leader was the dark Aryan god, Samana, head of the ancestral ghosts, also called the Lord of Death and the Grim Reaper. (*Pulls reaper out of sack*) The Feast of Samhain was held on October 31.

Sara: Oh, that was when the spirits came with their leader looking for their original homes, but if they couldn't find them, they looked for warm homes to enter since they'd been cold dead for so long.

Lin: Right, and if the people weren't nice to them and didn't "treat" them, what do you think might happen?

Sara: They'd probably get tricked by having their crops destroyed, their milk spilt or turned sour, or their lives made miserable. So what kind of treat did they offer?

Lin: (*Pulls out bread*) Food, their most valuable possession. Can you tell me, Sara, what usually happens around the end of October and the beginning of November?

Sara: I'm sure that the group can tell me what the farmers do at this time. (Harvest. *Pulls out bundle of wheat*)

Lin: Correct. Harvest time, the end of life, the beginning of death. I also remember from my geography that the autumn mists around these islands might suggest the visitation of spirits.

Sara: Right on. These people were very superstitious since they also paid homage to the ancient sun god who had ripened the grain which they now had safely stored away. Do you know who that sun god was they worshipped on October 31?

Lin: (*Pulls Bible out*) You'll find his name recorded in the Bible — Baal.

Sara: What does the Bible say about worshipping another god, Lin?

Lin: Don't do it! But people today are much like the nation of Israel who didn't listen. And because they worshipped pagan gods, Israel was sent into exile. Do you remember from the commandments what law this violated?

Sara: (*Holds up Commandment #1*) Thou shalt have no other gods but me. Hmm ... therefore, the origins of Halloween are based in the worshipping of pagan gods like Baal and Samana. Right?

Lin: Right, and when the Romans conquered the Celts in 43 A.D. they introduced these people into the ritual of honoring Pomona, the goddess of fruit and trees. Do any of you out there know what Halloween fruit might be associated with her? (*Pulls red apple out*)

Sara: Okay, group, and what do people do with this as they celebrate Halloween? (Answers: Bob for, tie on string, make cider and caramel apples)

Lin: Pagan beliefs like reincarnation also greatly influenced the celebration of this day. Can anyone tell me what that term means? (Answer: Belief that the souls of the dead return to earth in new forms or bodies.)

Sara: So pagans believe that when you die, your spirit goes to live in the body of an animal. Group, as Christians, do we believe this? (No.)

Lin: I have in my bag two such forms that pagans believe you might come back in. (*Pulls horse out*) First, as an evil pooka, a hideous black horse. The second, a cat. (*Pulls cat out*)

Sara: Now from my knowledge of ancient history, I remember that the cat was considered sacred by other religions: the Egyptians worshipped a cat-headed goddess called Pasht while the Greeks and Romans worshipped Hecate, a goddess who ruled over witches, wizards, and ghosts. Hecate's priestess was a cat who had once been a woman. Even the Norse honored Freya, a cat goddess of beauty, love, marriage, and death.

Lin: I can surely see where the cat got its superstitious reputation. People don't trust them because of their behavior. What does a black cat symbolize today, group? (Bad luck)

Sara: And no one wants bad luck, do they? I see from your book that there's another lesson to be learned about our origins of this day. Can anyone tell me what a "haunting" is? (When spirits frequent a place) According to history, villagers didn't want to have their villages haunted so they would dress up in masks and costumes to frighten these spirits away. These ancient "murmurs," as they were called, went from house to house collecting the ancient Celtic equivalent of protection money. Carrying jack-o-lanterns, they would then romp the ghosts out of town.

Lin: So, that's where the origins of trick or treating and carrying jack-o-lanterns came in? (*Pulls out jack-o-lantern*)

Sara: Right. The jack-o-lantern is a symbol of a damned soul. There's a legend about a man named Jack who couldn't enter heaven or hell. Having tricked the devil out of claiming his soul, but never really repenting, he'd been doomed to wander in the darkness for eternity. Hearing the man's laments, the devil tossed him a burning coal from hell which Jack caught in a turnip, and then proceeded to wander with this light until Judgment Day.

Lin: Interesting. So people began carving faces on pumpkins, turnips, and potatoes to frighten away all those nasty, evil spirits? (*Pulls out carved potato*)

Sara: Right. And ritual bonfires also surrounded a lot of this pagan ceremony. (*Pulls out poster of fire*) The villagers would relight their hearth fires which had been ritually extinguished at the end of every year from the flames of these bonfires. The light and heat from these fires were believed to help the sun make it through the cold, dark winter.

Lin: Now I like a cheery fire in my home, but I don't believe it helps the sun to survive.

Sara: Well, these people did. But as Christianity came into these areas, the fires were believed to protect Christians from the devil, the enemy of God and the church. The pagans, who once offered crops, animals, humans (often criminals and prisoners of war) into the flames of the fires, now had a different influence to consider.

Lin: The truth dawns! Instead of making sacrifices to the dead, the church established a day to remember the dead. Does anyone know what this is called and when it is? (All Saints' Day, November 1)

Sara: For Protestants this is a special day, for on October 31 Martin Luther posted his 95 Theses on the door of Wittenberg (*Pulls out scroll*) so that all who were coming to church on All Saints' Day would read them.

Lin: Do you know another name for All Saints' Day, group? (All Hallows) And what is October 31 known as in the church? (All Hallow's Eve, shortened to Halloween. *Pulls out sign with names written on both sides*)

Sara: According to history, the tenth century church set November 2 as All Souls' Day, a day to remember all the souls of the dead.

Lin: But people still look for supernatural excitement, don't they? I seem to recall that the people of that time became disgruntled with the regimentation and lack of excitement in the church and looked to other avenues of enlightenment.

Sara: Correct. They joined such groups as "Wicca." (*Pulls out witch hat*) "Wicca" is a Saxon word which means wise one, a wrong label for this group because witches seek to acquire greater knowledge through magic or witchcraft.

Lin: Others called sorcerers kept their magic "hidden" to retain their powers. Does anyone know what this "hidden" knowledge is called? (Occult. *Pulls out sign with "hidden" on one side and opens it to word "occult"*)

Sara: The occult is on the rise today for it suggests mystery, magic, and thoughts beyond the scope of understanding, and it lures many into astrology, numerology, divination and practices that the Word of God strictly speaks against.

Lin: Witches and magicians are often sought by many to foretell the future, aren't they? Does anyone remember the biblical king who sought out a witch to do this? (Saul/witch of Endor) Do you remember whom she summoned from the dead? (The prophet Samuel)

Sara: I remember she was really surprised for she didn't make contact with a spirit but with the real Samuel whom God allowed for that moment to return from the dead. But the Bible strictly tells us not to consult with the spirits of the dead. Do some people do this today? How? (Seance, a meeting of spiritualists to receive spirit communication)

Lin: Boy, people surely don't know what they're messing with as they pursue the spirit, do they?

Sara: No. For instance, a coven is a group of witches who perform magical rites and ceremonies and open themselves up to evil spirits. It's usually made up of 13, one master and 12 witches, and they hold sabbaths. (*Pulls out #13 sign*) What does the number 13 signify for many? (Bad luck)

Lin: What's a sabbath? (Day of rest and worship)

Sara: And Halloween is one of the four greater sabbaths which honor the Horned God of Hunting and Death. This is a harvest celebration in which it is believed that the Great Goddess goes to sleep for the long, winter months, giving way to this god who rules until her return May 1. This is a time of ritual, a time of ridding oneself of personal weakness, a time of feasting and celebration, a time of communing with the spirits of the dead.

Lin: Ah, another means to pull people from the truth. I can understand why the people of that time got so caught up in this. Many lived in poverty. Thousands would gather to celebrate this sabbath and make their dreary lives merry. Even members of royal families and the nobility often attended this celebration, concealing their faces by masks. (*Pulls mask out*)

Sara: (*Pulls out LAW card/scroll*) Ta da! Hear the law from the seventh century Archbishop of Canterbury, England, who hoped to guide those who had strayed from the truth by setting punishments for "those who goeth about in the masque of a stag or a bull-calf . . . those who by their craft raise storms . . . sacrifice to demons . . . consulteth soothsayers who divine by birds." In other words, those who worshipped the Horned God had better beware for they were in danger. If caught, they would be punished.

Lin: Yet people like to do their own thing. They continued to meet and dance around the bonfires dressed in animal skins and wearing the heads of animals, barking and howling and worshipping their god. Often they would straddle branches or other objects. Anyone guess what that might be? (*Pulls out broomstick*)

128

Sara: I see another object that they used here, too. (*Pulls ointment out*) Applying ointment to their skin, the witches would get a giddy feeling as the ointment numbed the skin, making them think they could actually fly.

Lin: Were there class distinctions with witches?

Sara: Oh, yes. Well-off witches rode horseback, but poor witches went on foot carrying brooms or poles to help them vault over brooks, streams, and thorny patches.

Lin: We often see pictures of witches stirring a cauldron. (*Pulls out spoon*) What is that, group? (A big cooking pot)

Sara: Here they would brew herbs to cure headaches, backaches, fevers and colds. They didn't have aspirin (*Pulls out bottle of aspirin*) and definitely didn't believe in the healing power of Christ. Also from this time there was another legendary group, especially related to Ireland, who hated the church. Do you remember who they were? (*Pulls out a doll representing the Little People*)

Lin: The Little People, whether a legend or actually a race of dark-skinned people from the Stone Age, were also called fairy folk or goblins. Like banshees, leprechauns, brownies, or pixies, they stand for the evil spirits that were once thought to emerge at Samhain and later on the eve of All Saints' Day, or Halloween. What color clothing did they wear, group? (Green, to help them hide in the forest. *Pulls out green clothing or hat*)

Sara: These folk weren't very nice, though. Often these dwarfs would waylay travellers, kidnap, and even murder. They shot at people and cattle with little arrows called elf bolts (*Pulls out lightning bolt*), and people began to use an iron object as a protective charm against these Little People. Anyone know what that is? (*Pulls out horseshoe*)

Lin: The crescent shape of this object was sacred to a pagan moon goddess. There was another iron object found in the steeples of many churches which the Little People despised. Can anyone guess what that might be? (Church bells — *Ring bell*)

Sara: On Halloween the church bells rang out loudly to keep the fairies at bay. But there are other things associated with Halloween I see you have in your bag yet.

Lin: (*Pulls out skeleton*) Yes, the skeleton, who makes us think of death. In Naples, Italy, on the eve of All Souls' Day the skeletons receive visitors in their tombs. Want to go visiting, Sara?

Sara: No thanks, Lin, but I also see a bat in your sack. (*Pulls out bat*) Can anyone tell us why it might be associated with Halloween? (Blood used for ointments by witches; entrails into brews; thought to have mysterious and evil powers)

Lin: Not much truth there. There are also some non-truths associated with a certain amphibian that goes "re-deep." Anyone know what that might be? (*Pulls out toad*) What superstitions are associated with it? (Cause warts or may be poisonous)

Sara: There are a lot of superstitions or irrational attitudes of the mind toward the supernatural, nature, or God, which come from ignorance, unreasoning fear of the unknown or the mysterious, which surround Halloween.

Lin: Yes. (*Pulls out salt shaker or box*) Like this salt. Salt and iron objects were often placed in the cradle of a newborn child to stop fairies and witches from carrying it off on Halloween night.

Sara: The Pennsylvania Dutch hung hex signs on their barn to ward off witches.

130

Lin: And I've seen some pretty colored ones. And speaking of color, what colors are associated with Halloween? (*Pulls orange paper out*) Orange represents strength and endurance and is symbolized most in ripened fruits, vegetables, and grains. (*Turns orange card over. LIFE written on back. Pulls out black card with DEATH written on back*) What does black symbolize? (Death) Life and death, an interesting truth, especially for the right spirit, right, Sara?

Sara: Right, and there are other things we use at this time of year which are associated with Halloween, like cornstalks, pumpkins, apples, apple cider, nuts, popcorn, and candy corn. They are all symbols of harvest and associated with Halloween. (*Pulls out apple and nuts*) In fact, nuts and apples were said to be able to tell your fortune. Do you think that is true, O great Lover of Truth?

Lin: Of course not. Only God knows the direction our lives are going. People who believe in superstitions are usually pursuing the wrong spirit. But even God's people get led astray in their ignorance and fleshly desires.

Sara: That's true. The ancient Hebrew women actually bathed in water mixed with the sap of the apple tree if they wanted a baby. (*Pulls out baby doll*)

Lin: Group, do you think this is a truth? (No) Yet the apple has been a token of love and fertility for ages. We all know the stork brings babies. Right, group?

Sara: Another superstition, but let's get back to Halloween. Superstitions cause us to seek truth in the wrong patch. For instance (*Pulls out cabbage*), unengaged people thought that by pulling kale or cabbage from the garden they would find out about their future mates.

Lin: What a trick! But this trick or treating ritual our kids do, how old is it?

Sara: Not that old. It evolved from children dressed up in costume going around to houses and asking for milk, eggs, cheese, corn or potatoes to ward off dangerous gods. Today it's give me "candy, candy, candy!" as Garfield would say. (*Pulls out Garfield cat with candy in hand or Trick or Treat bag*)

Lin: I know one costume that isn't true to the nature of the beast. It's that red-suited person. Do you know him, group? (Devil. *Pulls out red devil mask, trident, or figure*) Do we as Christians believe in the devil? (Yes)

Sara: We know the devil as one of God's created beings. Created as an angel of good, he chose to become evil. The Bible describes him as an angel of great beauty, but after his fall, he uses clever disguises as he works his evil among us.

Lin: A truth: Witches don't acknowledge the devil, but Satanists do. And do you know what Halloween is to Satanists?

Sara: I've heard it's celebrated as one of their two highest unholy days, a time to honor Satan and death, a day when everything God has called an "abomination" is glorified.

Lin: That is a terrible truth. They acknowledge the wrong lord of death. Who do we know that conquered death, group? (Jesus) How? (Defeated death on the cross and rose again. *Holds up cross*) Now that is real truth!

Sara: Well then, Lin, with all these truths we've uncovered, how should we as Christians celebrate Halloween?

Lin: We should spend our time rejoicing and claiming 1 John 3:8b: "The Son of God was revealed for this purpose, to destroy the works of the devil."

Sara: Good news! Therefore, we probably should be worshipping God that day and making intercession in prayer, especially for the children who are vulnerable to the spirits of fear and the occult.

Lin: Right, for Deuteronomy 18:10-11 strictly prohibits us as Christians from involvement in the occult and witchcraft. Another truth. So, toss out those tarot cards, that ouija board, those horoscopes, and the like.

Sara: (*Pulls out feather duster*) Looks like closet cleaning time, for 1 Thessalonians 5:22 reminds us to abstain from all appearances of evil. And Paul says, "Don't give any place to the devil" (Ephesians 4:27). Dress the kids as Care Bears, clowns, or princesses, not as devils. Christians are called to glorify God not Satan. Don't enter the dark side of Halloween, for Christ defeated the forces of darkness at Calvary. As Luke Skywalker used the force to defeat Darth Vader, we apply the Spirit, the blood of Christ, and the Cross to our lives to defeat darkness.

Lin: Right. And celebrate All Saint's Day, remembering those who have died, those Jesus purchased with his precious blood.

Sara: Right. For the saints of God are not doomed to roam this earth seeking the shelter and warmth of homes they once inhabited. They are warmed by the presence of their spirits with God in heaven where they feast at his banqueting table. They don't have to seek treats from souls here on earth, for God is their provider and no tricks! For with Jesus, there is only truth and no lie.

Lin: So, we need to be in pursuit of the right spirit in our lives. And what spirit is that, group? (The Holy Spirit. *Pulls out dove*)

Sara: So, let's go forth tonight and continue our search for all God has for us, and receive the Holy Ghost as a welcome visitor. As we open the doors of our hearts, we will let Jesus in. The Spirit of Christ will not violate or trick you, causing

133

fear through a haunting, for this spirit brings life, not death, in Jesus.

Lin: And that's the truth. Amen?

All: Amen and amen!

Carnival Games Option

If using this program as an alternative to a Halloween celebration, the following games may be used.

Ring The Candles: Use five canning jar rings. Participants throw at two tall candles set on a table. Three rings win a prize (candy/solicited prizes).

Paddle Bugs: Participants use a wooden paddle to hit six golf balls painted like bugs into coffee cans painted as bug traps. Prizes awarded for three balls in one can.

Where's The Spider? Paint three butter tubs black. Hide a rubber spider under one, and hide two other small, similar objects under the other two. Show the person. Then mix them up. Person needs to guess where the spider is hiding. Correct guess wins.

Pumpkin Toss: Toss three Frisbees painted black/orange into three covered boxes with attached pumpkin faces.

Pitch The Bat: Make three stuffed black bats to pitch into three baskets attached to chalk board.

Rattle My Bones: Throw three white dog chew bones at three 2-liter bottles painted black using sand for balance.

Choose A Clown's Nose: Attach inflated balloons to a white bedsheet strung out. Balloons have pieces of paper inside with prizes and scriptures listed. Solicit prizes from congregation (candy, bookmarks, and so forth). Use clown face with a blown-up balloon as a poster.

Sink The Pastor's Tonsils: Use a basketball ring attached to a poster of an open throat exposing tonsils. Paint three tennis balls red. Students throw three balls into hoop.

Tombstone Cake Walk: Number large tombstones and place on floor. Solicit cakes and cupcakes from congregation. Use music to move participants around. When music stops, the person over the tombstone with the number drawn wins. Have a large fish bowl to place the numbers in.

Cookie Decoration: Have Halloween cut-out cookies made. Use tubes to decorate with names.

Popcorn Treats: Put popcorn into bags decorated with Christian symbols and passages. Sunday school classes may be engaged in helping with this.

Make decorative posters advertising each game and place outside the classroom or by the game in the fellowship hall.

13

The Exodus Murmurers

Leader's Helps

This program may be used at any time during the year. It may be used for a women's group, youth event, or an intergenerational program. The focus is to help participants realize the dangers of complaining. Through a mock trial, three murmurers lay their complaints before the audience, their jury. A leader reflects on their arguments, and a court reporter uses the Bible and editorial comments to show that their accusations are not valid.

Set your stage as a courtroom. The three Exodus murmurers may come from the side grumbling and then seat themselves in the audience. The court reporter should be at a side table with her Bible and maybe some newsprint. A hat with "News" may be worn. As the witnesses are called, they take a chair to be examined and then return to their seats. The leader acts as a prosecuting attorney, the audience as jury.

Participants:
Leader
Court reporter
The Exodus Murmurers: Ms. Complaint, Ms. Grumble and
    Ms. Murmur

Program

Group: Complain, complain . . . grumble, grumble . . . murmur, murmur . . . .

Leader: What's that I hear? It sounds like a low, confused, indistinct sound, much like running water. Listen, there it goes again.

Group: Complain, complain . . . grumble, grumble . . . murmur, murmur . . . .

Leader: Now just who is doing that murmuring out there? Identify yourselves.

Group: We are the Exodus murmurers — Ms. Complaint, Ms. Grumble, and Ms. Murmur. We're hot and tired, and have a lot to murmur about. Complain, complain . . . grumble, grumble . . . murmur, murmur . . . .

Leader: Well, let's deal with you one at a time. Let's have you each take the stand and hear your tale. First, Ms. Complaint, what's your issue?

Ms. Complaint: I'd like to lodge a formal accusation against that leader of ours, Moses. Weren't there any graves down in Egypt that he had to lead us out into this wilderness to die? Just look at this place! All this sand and dust make me sick. I like warm weather, but this scorching heat is a bit much. And oh, the grief I am experiencing. It would have been better for us if Moses had left us alone. Serving the Egyptians was better than this lot we have in life now. Complain, complain, complain.

Leader: It does sound like you are quite discontented with your circumstances, Ms. Complaint. Let's ask our court reporter to bring out the historical evidence from the Bible so we can look a little closer at your lot. Those gathered here can examine it and be your jury.

Court reporter: In the Book of Exodus, I find quite a lengthy documentation of your nation's bondage in Egypt following the years of increased population growth. Under history, I see that Joseph, favored by Pharaoh, had died, and a new ruler took his place. Under occupational hazards, it looks like many of your people perished from forced labor. It states in the record that your cries to God for deliverance did not go unnoticed. Under leaders, I find that Moses and Aaron were sent by God to be his spokespersons before Pharaoh. Logged in spectacular happenings, we find a series of strange phenomena occurring. Yes, here they are all logged in the *Nile News,* a very accurate parchment news service: "Contest Wages Between Moses and Pharaoh" — staffs turning into snakes; water becoming blood; frogs; gnats; flies; livestock stricken; boils; hail and fire; locusts; darkness and light. Yes, proof that God was dramatically moving, making his presence known. And then the final blow happened: the death of the first born. That's when Pharaoh let you go. I guess your rejoicing soon turned to complaining when you looked at Pharaoh, his army and chariots pursuing you. That's when you turned so ungratefully on your leader. But it's noted here that Moses seemed to understand your fear. Maybe we can excuse your behavior because you hadn't walked with God for that long in order to really trust him. But proof is proof. How soon you forgot God's mighty deliverance!

Here's another headline from the *Wilderness Herald*: "People Turn on Leader, But No Retaliation." I'm glad to see that Moses didn't take this all personally. Often when we are overwhelmed by circumstances we lash out at others like you did. Understandable at times, but not in keeping with remembering God's power to overcome. God had taken you

139

out of slavery and set you free. But when you saw that the going was getting rough, you dug in your heels at the Red Sea and complained. That's all I have to report on my evidence concerning the accusations of Ms. Complaint.

Leader: It seems to me, Ms. Complaint, that Moses can serve as an example to you. What a humble witness! He did not become defensive or turn on you, accusing you of a lack of faith. No, instead, he offered encouragement. Hear his words again that he shared with you at the Red Sea: "Do not be afraid, stand firm, and see the deliverance that the Lord will accomplish for you today; for the Egyptians whom you see today you shall never see again. The Lord will fight for you, and you have only to keep still" (Exodus 14:13-14). Yet, that is difficult for many of us, isn't it? It's easier to complain about our circumstances than to keep quiet. But I recall from history that God came through and parted the Red Sea for you to cross through unharmed. When the armies pursued you, they were drowned. Then you praised God. That is to be credited to your account. But, this idea of quiet is hard for complainers. Being still is foreign to us, especially today in our chatter-filled world. Yet silence is an awesome proof of our faith in God. Silence speaks louder than words in defusing false accusations. There is a good example found in Mark 14 for us to recall as collaborating evidence. Court reporter, could you read that for us?

Court reporter: "Some stood up and gave false testimony against him, saying, 'We heard him say, "I will destroy this temple that is made with hands, and in three days I will build another, not made with hands." ' " (Mark 14:57-58).

Leader: Yes, often we will encounter folks who testify falsely. How should we then respond as Christians? Verses 60-61 from that same reading tell us how Jesus handled it.

Court reporter: "Then the high priest stood up before them and asked Jesus, 'Have you no answer? What is it that they testify against you?' But he was silent and did not answer."

140

Leader: It is recorded, Ms. Complaint, that you and your company complained and prayed to God for years about your condition. Yet, there seems to be overwhelming proof that God heard your cries, delivered you, and led you into the wilderness. However, instead of looking at your wilderness experience as a growing time where faith could be solidified, I fear you turned it into a time to murmur. Moses then had to give you an attitude adjustment and correct your faulty logic. Saint Peter tells us how to do this also. Court reporter, could we hear that passage?

Court reporter: Hebrews 12:5b-7 states: "My child, do not regard lightly the discipline of the Lord, or lose heart when you are punished by him; for the Lord disciplines those whom he loves, and chastises every child whom he accepts. Endure trials for the sake of discipline. God is treating you as children; for what child is there whom a parent does not discipline?"

Leader: I wonder? Did you hear Moses' advice to stand firm, trust in God, be still and see how God would work things out for you? Hmmm ... You are dismissed for now.

Ms. Grumble: Grumble, grumble ... growl, growl ... snap, snap ....

Leader: Well, I think we are about to hear from our next Exodus murmurer, Ms. Grumble. Sit down here, and speak loudly so all can hear. What's your story, my dear?

Ms. Grumble: I, too, would just like to lodge my complaint with this court. Three days! Three days — we walked without water. Three days with nothing to quench our thirst. Then, when we got to that place called Marah, we thought we'd be refreshed. And what did we get to drink? Bitter water. No lemonade stands in this desert. No pop machines. No automatic bubblers. Now tell me, who wouldn't grumble about that?

Leader: Okay, I can understand your thirst, but let's hear what our court reporter found in the Word of God to see if your grumbling is justified.

Court reporter: I found in Exodus 15 where God showed Moses a piece of wood, which when thrown into the bitter water, made that water become sweet. Treating this incident symbolically, we might wonder if there is any tree which, when thrown into the bitter waters of life, will make them sweet. As an editorial comment, often we find in our wilderness wanderings that the waters of life are sometimes bitter. Nothing seems to sweeten them, and we grumble about our lot. That's when the person of our Lord Jesus Christ becomes that piece of wood which can sweeten our tainted lives. He can help us to drink bitter waters without becoming embittered ourselves. John 4:14 states that Jesus said, "Those who drink of the water that I will give them will never be thirsty. The water that I will give will become in them a spring of water gushing up to eternal life."

Leader: And I remember more from that chapter, Ms. Grumble. The Lord heard your murmuring and made a statute and ordinance, and also put you to the test. If you would listen carefully to God's voice, and do what was right in his sight, and heed his commandments, then you would never suffer any of the diseases that he brought upon the Egyptians. What a deal! That's a promise from God to us today. Yet, God's own elect so often, in the midst of suffering and conflict, cry out day and night. Grumbling often occurs when we lose patience. You lost it after only three days. Some may lose it over a longer period of time. Sometimes prayers are not answered as quickly as we would like, and we begin to murmur that God hasn't heard our cries. We become bitter. The Father has the times and seasons in his hands. He alone knows the moment when a soul or church is ripened to the fullness of faith so it can really take and keep the blessing he will bestow. God was at work at Marah training you with the bitter. He may be at work in us right now asking us to stop our grumbling and allow him to sweeten our lives. As parents long to have their children mature, and yet wait patiently until the time of training is completed, so it is with God and his children. He is the long-suffering one who answers speedily. He is the one who sees if we will apply the Cross to the bitterness of sin in our lives and allow Christ to heal us. Sin is the greatest obstacle to unanswered prayer. The root of bitterness and grumbling about life has to be dug up and thrown into the fires. It is a destructive weapon to our faith. A killer to spiritual growth. It seems to me that the evidence in the Bible shows us that the Israelites' faith in God to do as he promised never went beyond the next obstacle. First, they complained in the wilderness as they looked at their circumstances and forgot what God had already done for them. Next, they thirsted and didn't like the water God gave to drink. Now we hear from our last witness, Ms. Murmur. Please, take the stand.

Ms. Murmur: Complain, complain ... grumble, grumble ... murmur, murmur ... (*Very low*).

Leader: Speak up, Ms. Murmur. I can hardly hear you.

Ms. Murmur: Well, murmuring is best done in low mutterings so that you can hardly make it out. Now, I don't want you or this fine jury to think I'm stubborn or refused to journey, but I had to put my foot down with an obstinate stamp. (*Stamps foot*) Just tell me, how can anyone survive without meat or bread? We had our fill of things to eat in Egypt, but out there in the wilderness, we were starving!

Leader: Let's have our court reporter look up the facts here, Ms. Murmur.

Court reporter: (*Thumbs through Bible*) Hmmm ... yes, I see your murmuring was referred to eight times in the first 12 verses of Exodus 16. This is serious — it seems to be more than just grumbling or complaining. It looks like your constant grumbling, that is your stubbornness and refusal to continue under

143

God's direction, had dire consequences. It's recorded here that you weren't just murmuring against Moses but against God. Even when God provided quail and manna, you still didn't stop. As another observation, I would think that you would have ceased all your complaining, grumbling, and murmuring and trusted God to keep his promises. But no, the record shows that your lack of trust cost you a wandering of 40 years in the desert. That was a life span for a person then. In fact, from that group all who grumbled and complained against the Lord did not receive entry into the Promised Land. They spent their lives not accepting the blessings God had in store for them. However, there were two exceptions found in the Book of Numbers and reported in the *Canaan Chronicler,* under the story, "Spies Reported in Land of Promise." Caleb and Joshua didn't murmur when they saw overwhelming obstacles. They gave a good report to the people concerning the feasibility of occupying the land God had promised them, but they were the minority opinion.

Leader: And so you murmurers chose to grumble against God and the odds of taking the land of Canaan. The abundant life that awaited you, you would not step out and claim. The rest is history. Please, step down now, Ms. Murmur.

Well, jury, you've heard the complaints of these three murmurers. In summation, I would like to point out that they chose death instead of life. Their sin of murmuring evidenced an unwillingness to follow God. The root of the Hebrew word for murmur is "stop," and stop they did. They did not trust God to defeat their enemies, provide for their needs, or see to their welfare. Instead, they murmured every step of the way. They stopped seeing how God was at work in their lives. Their memories of his faithfulness were short-lived. Consequently, their sentence was that they never experienced the satisfaction of fulfilling God's purpose. They were so intent on having their immediate needs met that they always found fault and murmured when faced with each new problem.

Israel seemed to be a nation of habitual complainers. Some people today might fall into that category. Like our three sisters here, many complain about anything and everything until, without realizing it, they have developed a bitter, ungrateful attitude. How "I"-centered they become. Every thought of unbelief in the wisdom and goodness of God is evidence of self-centered persons who believe that they — not God — should control the affairs of their lives. Granted, it may seem at times that God has not met our needs, that is not met them the way we think he should. But praising God during times of testing always honors him and is the key to victory in receiving blessings from him. 1 Thessalonians 5:18 tells us to "give thanks in all circumstances; for this is the will of God in Christ Jesus for you." When times of trial come, we stand on 1 Peter 5:10 that says, "After you have suffered for a little while, the God of grace, who has called you to his eternal glory in Christ, will himself restore, support, strengthen, and establish you."

Murmurers, most of your troubles, and ours, happen because of our own foolish mistakes — not by our faithfulness to God. Then we suffer the consequences. Yet there are times when Christians suffer for their stand for Christ. The precious purpose of suffering is to make us perfect, to establish us, and to strengthen and settle us. Trials don't come by accident, but by God's appointment or permission as seen with Job. God knows exactly what we need, and he never makes a mistake in the time, place, or type of trial we need in order to perfect his purpose in us. Rejoicing in the Lord calls us at times to rejoice in tribulation. When we walk under bondage, however, we are not free to do this. You murmurers were set free from the physical bondage of slavery in Egypt but traveled with a lot of baggage in your spiritual lives. The walk of faith God led you on was to develop your trust in him to provide for you. As we become less preoccupied with present problems and are submissive to God's leading, we will have our deliverance. Circumstances that seem bleak cause us to lose our self-confidence, our self-sufficiency, and lead us to greater dependence on the Almighty. God is always at work in us, establishing a trust factor. When we are the weakest, Saint Paul reminds us, God is the strongest. What a growth point when we understand this: When we are the least powerful, God is the most powerful. There are no short cuts in spiritual growth, but often we seek them.

Court reporter: Israel sought short cuts to spiritual maturity evidenced in their murmuring. God desires us to grow up in Christ and trust him to walk through difficulties with us. We are led out of bondage only through Christ. Sometimes negative situations can be seen as positive learning experiences. But when we murmur about them, they become unfavorable points of friction between us and God. There is no peace for murmurers. There is no hope in their hearts. They only see what they espouse in complaints, grumblings, and murmurings. Their hearts are not yielded to God and his purpose.

Leader: Hearts dedicated and yielded to Christ will cease their murmuring and complaining. Faith that does not stop when the going gets rough will send up praise to God and declare, "Whatsoever pleases thee, Lord, pleases me."

May all we utter please our Lord. May our complaining, grumbling, and murmuring cease so that we truly will glorify the God who is at work in our midst. God will forgive us and take away our guilt if we have sinned in this area. For our desire to grow will only be hindered by our hanging on.

Exodus murmurers, how do you plead?

Group: Guilty, but forgive us.

Leader: Through Christ you have been forgiven. Punishment has been paid. Jesus died in your place. In God's mercy receive full pardon for your sin. We rest in God's grace. Amen and amen.

14

Where Do I Belong?

Leader's Helps

"Where Do I Belong?" is a program designed to explore the reasons women belong to their church's women's organization. This program may be adapted to the local congregation or denominational group, and personalized in those areas where desired.

Participants include: Wanda, the traveling "Women of the Church" (insert your church body's name) reporter; an actress; a senior citizen; a bowler; and Connie Upreach, a congregational unit member (five person cast).

Props for each woman are suggested. Choose participants who like to ham it up. This is an excellent resource to help recruit new members and to encourage faithful ones. Feel free to adapt to the local, regional, and national situations.

Program

Wanda: (*Enters left carrying a notebook and pencil, looking bewildered about where she should be*) Hello! Hello! Is anybody there? Let's see. I'm trying to figure out where I belong. Let me check my schedule. (*Opens notebook and nods*) Yes. I'm where I'm supposed to be. (Name of congregation, address, city, state) Yes, here is where I'm supposed to be. (*Looks at audience*) And there you are! Hello! Are you where you belong? Let me introduce myself. I'm Wanda, the traveling "Women of the Church" reporter. I've come from our Church-wide Organization in (city) to spend some time with you. Our executive director (name) sent me here to ask your ladies why they belong to that organization. All of you women out there belong, right? Silly question. Of course, you do, and if you don't I'm sure you have heard of this group. Well, let's go see what "belonging" is all about. Come on along. (*Moves center stage*)

(*Actress enters opposite end of stage. Wanda moves over to question her. She carries a handful of newspapers and papers*)

Wanda: Hello there. I'm Wanda, the traveling "Women of the Church" reporter. I'd like to ask you why you belong to the congregational unit of the women's organization here at your church.

Actress: Sorry . . . You're asking the wrong person. You should locate Constance Upreach. We call her CU for short. Connie's involved in all that women's stuff. Me . . . I'm into communication and leading. I belong to the local acting group in our community. We put on a lot of different entertainment for our local people. CU's always trying to get me to come and present a program for this unit, but I just don't have the time. Good people are always in demand, and I'm good, you know. In fact, we're looking at doing the play *Chicago* next season. I might just land the leading role. However, I can already see the churchy ladies blush when I strut out on stage singing "All That Jazz!" (*Pulls garter from purse and waves around*) My short skirt would expose a lot of leg, and I'm sure they wouldn't approve of some of the language that's used. No, let Connie communicate her way, and I'll witness in my own.

Wanda: Well, what about your witness of faith? If you're a star, I'm sure that you'd make a good program leader some time.

Actress: That's what CU's always saying. I witnessed my faith last season. We did *Agnes of God* and I played the Mother Superior.

Wanda: Did you learn anything about the Catholic faith from this "learning" experience?

Actress: That's what Connie asked me when she invited me to an ecumenical service for the World Day of Prayer. But, I didn't have time to go. You know learning a script takes a lot of memorization, and then there are all those rehearsals. After all, belonging to a group like that is a big commitment. And I'm really committed to acting. Commitment is where it's at, and I do really well. Just look at all my reviews. (*Stuffs a bunch of papers in Wanda's hand and rushes off stage*) Keep them! I have plenty. 'Bye now! Have to chat with the girls at the coffee hour about putting on a skit for a fund raiser.

Wanda: (*Turns to congregation and writes in notebook*) Well, belonging involves active participation and commitment. Leadership skills, communication, witness — these are important items for that lady. Those areas are foundational to growth in our organization also. I'll have to spur that Constance

149

Upreach to contact that lady and tap all that "potential." We just have to find the right avenues in this group to develop that woman as a whole person. But wait! Here comes another good prospect for interviewing.

Senior Citizen: (*Enters carrying a suitcase with labels*) Hi there, Sweetie! Do you belong here? I haven't noticed you before, and I've been a member for a looooooooong time!

Wanda: No. I'm Wanda, the traveling "Women of the Church" reporter sent out by the Church-wide Organization to find out why you belong to the congregational unit of this church.

Senior Citizen: Oh, I don't belong. You want Constance Upreach. CU for short. She's really active in that group. She's always trying to get me to come to some of their events, but I belong to our Senior Citizens' group. We meet twice a month, eat, play bingo and cards, and take lots of trips. I have stickers for all the places we've been to on my suitcase. See! Last summer we went to the museum of science and industry in (place). This fall we took a color tour around (place). You should join us. See this sticker? It's to our local historical museum. Lots of interesting stuff right in our own backyard.

Wanda: Yes, I agree on that, but it is good to have a wider vision of things around you. Speaking of vision, that's what your women do when they attend national gatherings. Did you know that there is a large group of women from all over the country that attends our national women's convention in some great spots in this nation? The next one will be in (year) in (place). Your women will be electing delegates to go to that. You should think about being a nominee.

Senior Citizen: Wow! (Point of interest in the city) is there. I bet they have some great stickers. If I was a delegate, but . . . my age. I'm sure they wouldn't want an old lady like me to go as their representative.

Wanda: Our women's group is made up of all ages, and each age has many gifts to offer. Have you ever been to any of our women's retreats or camping experiences?

Senior Citizen: I see them advertised a lot, and Connie's always trying to get me to go. CU says I should take my fall color tour and some time for God at the next Fall Retreat. I heard they do some great things to relieve stress. Even had nuns singing from *Sister Act* one time. I should tell my actress friend about that group. I heard that women my age add a lot of spice to some of those sessions. We are quite experienced, you know, but I go to my daughter's in June. Visit my grandkids. That's important.

Wanda: Ever think of taking them with you to camp? They have a great children's ministry. What a gift you'd give them and yourself. See if your church offers some scholarships.

Senior Citizen: They might. If they don't, I should encourage them to do that. We seniors like our discounts. I'll have to think about that. Some of the women in my Senior Citizen's group do put those retreats on their priority list. They've encouraged me to take better care of myself and have invited me to come with them, to pull apart from all my busyness. I tend to overdo at times. Definitely affects the old body. Hmmm ... I'll have to think about all you've said. There are a lot of outings that I can go to. Want to see my pictures? I have a whole album. Here (*Shoves photo album in her hands*). I'll pick it up after the coffee hour. Need to go show the women my latest pics of the grandkids.

Wanda: (*Takes out notebook*) Belonging — fellowship opportunities, stewardship of self, travel, strengthening the whole person. The needs of that woman can be met by our organization as we help her grow and build community with others. Have to pray she makes contact with that Constance Upreach. I need another interviewee, and here she comes.

Bowler: (*Enters carrying a bowling bag*) Hello. Just want to grab a quick cup of coffee before my game. I'm on the Church League. We bowl after service each Sunday. I've tried to get the area pastors to join. But they are always arranging some fellowship thing on Sundays. Imagine ... today they'd rather be working with kids or visiting the hospitals or doing a Bible study than bowling. But me, I love bowling. Belong to a weekly afternoon group, too. Do you bowl? I have a pretty decent average, if I do say so myself.

Wanda: I've bowled for fun with some of my friends from church and our youth group, but let me introduce myself. I'm Wanda, the traveling "Women of the Church" reporter. I'm here to find out why you belong to your women's organization.

Bowler: You want Constance Upreach. CU for short. She's been after me for years to come to their afternoon circle meetings, but that's when I bowl. She's tried to get me to switch leagues, but I've been with this one for ever so long. I'm a powerhouse for them. It would mean ordering a new jacket. We have team names, you know. We're the Purple Power Persons, PPPs for short.

Wanda: Power is important today, but what about empowering your faith? If you're developing your bowling skills, surely a "wise" woman like yourself would like to improve her study and reflection average, also. As a team member of this group, your theological growth is important.

Bowler: Yeah, I've heard that line before. Connie invited me to an area event, but I have an out-of-town bowling tournament on that weekend. Some of the women are really excited about going to hear about what's happening at all levels in their organization.

Wanda: Those are special times with Bible study and workshops. That type of event equips women for ministry. Have you ever shared the good news of your faith with the other women on your team?

Bowler: They know I go to church. Just ask anyone here. But I don't know that much about faith stuff. I suppose I could go to that morning circle instead of switching leagues. They're doing that new women's Bible study. Hmmm ... do they give trophies for that?

Wanda: Not like bowling, but when you see him, God will present you with a trophy for taking time out to learn more about him.

Bowler: Well, you've given me a lot to think about. I've felt distant from God for a time now. Not much power in my life in that area. But, boy, do I have good form and a dynamite delivery when I bowl. Made lots of strikes last night, and some fantastic spares! Hope I do as well this afternoon. Have to run now. This group is special, church women you know. Won the league trophy last week. Check it out in the trophy case! 'Bye now.

Wanda: (*Writes in notebook*) Need for study and reflection. Need to grow theologically. Need to be equipped with power. Team participation. Hey, these are aims that our women's group uses to help us with growth, to build community, and to take action. Three great areas for everyone to be working on. I'll have to tell Connie about that lady.

Constance Upreach: (*Enters carrying Bible, copy of women's magazine, a program resource book*) Good morning. I'm Constance Upreach. Just call me CU for short! I belong to this church, great place, and I am a member of its women's organization. We're having an informational meeting during the coffee hour about our latest action project in the community. You know the purposes of our missions overlap quite a bit. Belonging to that group has helped me grow so much. Do you belong here?

Wanda: I'm Wanda, the traveling "Women of the Church" reporter, and I've been asking the women here at (name of church) why they belong to your women's organization.

Connie: It's a fantastic group for me. I've done so much this year already in growing personally. We've had some terrific programs and events. I went to our big (synod, region, etc.) convention at (place) and heard some great speakers and networked with a lot of our women. Great fellowship and a wonderful learning experience. Spiritually renewing.

Wanda: Did you attend your camping programs I've heard so much about?

Connie: Yes. The chaplain was fantastic. Very well prepared. Fit in so well, and all the ladies loved (her/him). The kids had great care. The Fall Retreat gave us a lot to think about. And do you know, they had a great number of first-timers there. Everyone made them feel most welcome.

Wanda: Well, I'm sure they went home fired up and ready to tell others of their welcome. Positive experiences like those help women to see the value in our organization and give others encouragement to continue in participating.

Connie: Yes, those times challenge all of us to be active in our local units, to be committed in our faith, and to build community as sisters in Christ.

Wanda: All three areas of great potential and mission for the women of the church. On a personal note, from the reports I've heard, you certainly take advantage of belonging to this women's organization.

Connie: There is so much that one can get committed to in this organization. I feel so blessed to be able to support it and be as involved as I want and to grow in all areas. No one pushes, but the programs and fellowship draw many in. Our theme for the next (number) years will be (theme) with an emphasis on (emphasis). There's so much we can do to give others hope. Well, have to go now. I'm leading a forum on some of the things we at (local church) can do to nurture our faith in Christ through the women of the church this year. There are three women in particular I want to get involved. Bowling's over, no scheduled trips, and the play has not been chosen. Yes, those three should be free to think about a commitment right now. It was nice talking to you. Oh, ladies, grab a cup of coffee and come hear the great ideas I have for us to share in. (*Runs off waving*)

Wanda: Well, I think I have enough information on why women belong to our organization. Do you know where you belong? This organization involves the men in many intergenerational events also. I've even heard of some men quilting and cooking for various events. For me, and I hope for you, this organization is right where I belong. I'll just write all this up, and maybe you'll read about yourselves in (name of national magazine). See you next year, folks. 'Bye now.

15

Women Bearing Gifts

Leader's Helps

"Women Bearing Gifts" may be used in two ways to celebrate the Advent Season:
1) As a mid-week Advent worship;
2) As a women's or intergenerational Advent or Christmas program.
This worship service includes six participants: a worship leader and five narrators (Tamar, Rahab, Ruth, Bathsheba, and Mary).

Outline Of The Service
1. **The Gift Of Worship:** Invocation and carol.
2. **The Gift Of Adoration:** A litany based on Psalm 76.
3. **The Gift Of Confession:** Call to confess, silent confession, and the Lord's Prayer.
4. **Women Bearing Gifts:** Each section is introduced by the leader. Each woman reads the passage and then her part. The Gift of Righteousness — Tamar, The Gift of Trust — Rahab, The Gift of Unselfish Love — Ruth, The Gift of Repentance — Bathsheba, and The Gift of Obedience — Mary. Each section closes with a hymn.
5. **Bring Your Gifts To The Manger:** Insert in the bulletin slips of paper addressed to Jesus (Example: To Jesus, I present the gift of _____). During a special musical presentation, the participants will write a gift they wish to present to Christ and sign their papers. As the offering is taken, they will include these papers with it. An offertory prayer is made.

157

*Option: At this point, if there is a purpose statement to the women's organization, this may be inserted and said together.

A benediction is said, and the worship closes with a carol.

Verses of musical selections may be added or deleted as wished.

Program

An Advent/Christmas Celebration

The Gift Of Worship

*Invocation:

L: We call upon the Lord God to be present as we join our hearts in celebration. Pour forth your Spirit, O Holy One, that we might honor the Christ Child with our gifts of love and praise.

C: ACCEPT OUR OFFERING OF WORSHIP. AMEN.

*Opening Carol: "What Child Is This?"

The Gift Of Adoration

(A Litany Based on Psalm 76)

L: In Judah God is known, his name is great in Israel.

C: YOUR NAME IS GREAT, ALL MIGHTY GOD. WE BEAR THE NAME CHRISTIAN AS YOUR GIFT.

L: Glorious are you, more majestic than the everlasting mountains.

C: YOUR MAJESTY IS ABOVE THE HEAVENS, ALL GLORIOUS GOD. WE ARE IN AWE OF THE GIFT OF CREATION.

L: But you indeed are awesome! Who can stand before you when once your anger is roused?

C: YOUR FORGIVENESS IS WELCOMED, ALL MER-CIFUL GOD. WE REJOICE IN THE GIFT OF GRACE.

L: Make vows to the Lord your God, and perform them; let all who are around him bring gifts to the one who is awesome.

C: OUR GOD IS AN AWESOME GOD WHO SENT US THE GIFT OF SALVATION. WE CELEBRATE THE CHRIST CHILD THIS NIGHT BY OFFERING GOD OUR GIFT OF WORSHIP. AMEN.

The Gift Of Confession

L: As we gather in this special time of celebration, we recognize the gift that God sent to the world as a child. Jesus emptied himself of his glory in heaven and entered our world, taking the form of a slave and being born in human likeness. He shared with us the gifts of humility and obedience which cost him his life, given as salvation for the world. Because of that gift, God has exalted him. We honor Christ's name, bending our knee in adoration and with tongues confessing that Jesus Christ is Lord, to the glory of God the Father.

C: WE CONFESS OUR SINS TO YOU, ALMIGHTY GOD, AND CONFESS OUR NEED OF THE SAVIOR.

(*Silent confession*)

Leader: Receive pardon and forgiveness from the Child of Bethlehem. Let us pray the prayer that binds us in that grace.

*The Lord's Prayer

Women Bearing Gifts

Leader: Tonight we will hear from the women of the past who bring to the manger gifts which honor the Son of God. As you listen to them, ponder if you can bring that gift to Jesus this season. Let us hear from our first woman, Tamar, who brings the Gift of Righteousness.

The Gift Of Righteousness As Presented By Tamar

Reading: 2 Timothy 2:19-26

Tamar: Righteousness — that's what I was looking to Judah to give me as a gift. Instead I had to resort to trickery to be made right. I wasn't a wicked woman, but I certainly had things happen to me that made me question. My first husband, Er, was a brute and did not treat me right. When he died, as was our custom, I was given to his brother to ensure an heir. Now Onan wasn't much better. So when he died, I lived childless and a widow for some time. The last brother, Shelah, was too young for me, but I think Judah, my father-in-law, was really worried that Shelah would end up dead like his brothers if he entered my bed. What a reputation I had in our community, and I had done nothing wrong! So, I didn't feel one bit guilty about tricking Judah into laying with me in order to conceive a child. Shelah had grown up, but Judah had not given me to him as his wife. So, after taking Judah's seal and cord as a pledge, I slept with my father-in-law. Of course, when he found out I was pregnant, he was irate. But pulling out his pledge, I showed him that he was the father of my child. Judah then recognized my gift, declaring me more righteous than himself. When it came time for me to deliver, twins came forth — a double blessing. A scarlet thread was tied on the hand of the first, Zerah, but he drew back to let his brother, Perez, come forth. It is from Perez that the line of the Messiah came. God made things right for me in my situation. God made the selection right of a descendant of Christ. The scarlet thread reminds us of the blood of Christ tied to each of us as we become heirs to the promise of becoming children of righteousness. God made things right with the death of Jesus. He calls us through that righteousness to present to him upright lives. And so, we come to the manger and bear that gift — holy lives — lives made right by Christ's gift to us. Our hope rests in Christ, his oath, his covenant, his blood. Judah recognized my righteousness and clothed me in his name to bear my children. I recognize the righteousness I have to offer is not my own, but a gift from God. Join me in declaring that gift through song.

Hymn: "My Hope Is Built On Nothing Less" (v. 1)

Leader: As Tamar brought her gift to God and in return became part of the ancestry of Jesus, let us hear from another of that line, Rahab, who brings the Gift of Trust.

The Gift Of Trust As Presented By Rahab

Reading: Psalm 9:1-10

Rahab: The psalm that I just read was written after my time by King David, but he and I have a lot in common. Enemies surrounded us. Now for me, it was that nation called Israel that had come up from out of Egypt, an enemy I had heard plenty about. These people had put their trust in a God who brought them out of slavery. Yet they had rebelled against that God in the wilderness and found themselves wandering about for 40 years. But even then their God was with them. Now they had crossed the Jordan, trusting in that same God to give them this Promised Land. Well, here they were standing before the gates of my city, Jericho. I had to make a choice — trust in my city's forces to defend me, trust in myself and the profession of harlot to endear me to the enemy, or throw myself on the mercy of this God and his people and trust that my household would be saved. I had nothing to offer this God. My city was very ungodly. My profession was not very pure. The people I lived with were hopelessly depraved. Trusting in them to defend me was really laughable. Why shouldn't this God destroy this city? They were only interested in pursuing pleasure and indulging in sin. When those spies came to my house, I saw my chance. I offered them the gift of secrecy and protection in exchange for sparing my family. They commanded me to tie a scarlet cord in my window as a sign to their forces to spare me. Standing before you in your time, I see clearly God's hand in choosing to save me. I was the most unlikely candidate for this gift of salvation. Yet, by putting my trust in this God I did not know, I was blessed. I believed God would destroy Jericho and trusted in that scarlet cord and the gift I offered God's people. Because of that trust, I was saved and became an ancestor to the Child you honor tonight. Jesus' own blood became the scarlet cord which binds us together in faith. So bring your Gift of Trust to the manger this night and declare your faith in Christ to save. My town was sinful and fell to judgment. Join me in singing of the town where salvation was born as you declare your trust in God to deliver.

Carol: "O Little Town Of Bethlehem" (v. 1)

Leader: Tamar and Rahab, women bearing gifts to the Christ Child of Bethlehem. There is another from that line who brought a Gift of Unselfish Love. Let us hear from our third visitor, Ruth.

The Gift Of Unselfish Love As Presented By Ruth

Reading: 1 Corinthians 13:1-13

Ruth: I never thought of myself in the way this passage describes love. I just loved. My mother-in-law needed me. She faced a lonely life without her husband and sons. I do not hold it against my sister-in-law for returning to her people. I just couldn't abandon Naomi. I chose to let her people be my people and her God become mine also. I only heard about him as I listened to the scriptures read around our table and witnessed of him as I lived in that community. I gave my love to Naomi because she was family. I did not question her desire to give me to Boaz and allow him to become my kinsman-redeemer. I respected her wishes and trusted in this God who was caring for us. Bethlehem became not only my home as a widow, but my home as a wife. What a celebration that city had as Boaz and I were wed! How we rejoiced as I gave birth to a son, Obed! Little did I know then that he would be the father of Jesse, who would be the father of King David, from whom Jesus would come. I was honored by God to be part of this plan. As a Gentile, I see now God's plan of salvation for all people. As we offer the world the Gift of Unselfish Love we have found in Jesus, all nations will hail him as king and sing the wonders of his love. Join me now in declaring the joy we have as we bring to the manger the Gift of Unselfish Love.

Carol: "Joy To The World" (vv. 1 and 2)

Leader: Our next visitor is referred to in the genealogy of Jesus as Uriah's wife. We know this woman to be Bathsheba. She brings to the manger the Gift of Repentance. Let us hear her story.

The Gift Of Repentance As Presented By Bathsheba

Reading: John 8:3-11

Bathsheba: It wasn't my fault, and yet I was part of the temptation that led David to sin. I should have been more careful that night as I took my bath. I was beautiful, and at times I flaunted that beauty. Little did I know that the king would be gazing down upon me from his rooftop. When the soldiers came to take me to him, I could have resisted, but pride got in my way. I was flattered to be sought by the king for the night. I could have reminded him that we were sinning with our action, but again, I let my flesh get in the way. If I had been honest with Uriah and told him everything in a letter, he might be alive today. He may have forgiven David and charged him, but I compounded our sin by my silence. After Uriah's death, David took me as his wife, but our joy soon turned into grief when our child died. We were heartbroken, but both of us received God's grace as we turned to him in repentance.

164

Nathan reminded David of his action, and the king threw himself on the mercy of God. I followed suit, unable to bear the weight of guilt alone. God was so good in flooding my soul with peace and planting life anew with another son, Solomon. His name means "loved by the Lord." When we bring our Gift of Repentance to the Christ Child, we know what it means to be loved by the Lord. As we gaze upon Jesus, the Son God so loved, we know what it cost the Father for our sins. And so, we offer to Jesus the Gift of Repentance and embrace the gift of God's forgiveness. I found that gift when I turned to God and received his love. Join me now in declaring the Father's love for each of us, his repentant and now faithful children.

Carol: "Oh, Come All Ye Faithful" (v. 1)

Leader: Tamar, Rahab, Ruth, Uriah's wife, all listed in Jesus' lineage from Matthew. The last woman mentioned there is Mary, the mother of our Lord and Savior, who brings to us tonight the Gift of Obedience. Let us hear from our final woman who bears us a special gift.

The Gift Of Obedience As Presented By Mary

Reading: Matthew 12:46-50

Mary: When the angel came to me and told me I would be the mother of the Messiah, I was awestruck. Every Hebrew maiden found the prospect of being the Savior's mother something to be desired. What a wonderful thing to be so highly favored in God's eyes! Yet how could it be? I was a virgin. How the tongues would wag! And Joseph, my beloved, what would he think of me? All these thoughts bounced around in my mind as I listened to the angel tell me I would have a son who would be given the throne of his father David. My child, he declared, would reign over the house of Jacob forever; his kingdom would never end. Yet even with this promise, I still

165

wondered how this could happen. The angel reminded me that with God nothing is impossible. Therefore, I gave my Gift of Obedience consenting to God's will. All who hear God and obey do the Father's will. Often we hear God but choose not to follow through on his direction. Sometimes we doubt God is able to do what has been promised. Remember me then. God is faithful, and as we obey him, we find favor in his sight. As I gazed at my son, born that night in a stable, I rejoiced in the Gift of Obedience that allowed me to give my consent to God for his will to be done. May you surrender your will to Jesus that you may be his brother, his sister, his mother. Give Christ the Gift of Obedience this Christmas. I heard the angel and believed. Hear the angels from on high, and join me in singing praises to the newborn king.

Carol: "Angels We Have Heard On High"

Bring Your Gifts To The Manger

Leader: Included in your bulletin is a slip of paper. Take this time now to reflect on the gifts that have been spoken of tonight. Remember the women who bore them: Tamar and the Gift of Righteousness, Rahab and the Gift of Trust, Ruth and the Gift of Unselfish Love, Bathsheba and the Gift of Repentance, Mary and the Gift of Obedience. Think of God's greatest gift, Jesus, the Gift of Salvation. Then write down the gift you would bring to the manger this night and place it with your offering in the plate which will be passed around.

(*Time for reflection*)

Special Musical Gift And Offering

*Offertory Prayer
Leader: All Loving Father, we offer up to you our gifts knowing that you will take them as but tokens of the love we bear

your Son, Jesus. Before the manger of the Christ Child we bow and give thanks to you for the opportunity to return but a portion of all that you have blessed us with. Receive this offering in the name of the Babe of Bethlehem, through whom we pray.

All: Amen.

*Benediction
Leader: Go forth in love as children of God, bearing gifts to the world in Jesus' name and be a blessing to all nations. In the name of the Father, who sent the Son, Jesus, who gave us his Spirit to sing forth our noels.

*Closing Carol: "The First Noel"